This book is given to

_____

on this day

_____

T0054208

Keeping *Hope* Alive

Devotions for Strength in the Storm

GRACE FOX

AspirePress

Keeping Hope Alive: Devotions for Strength in the Storm
Copyright © 2022 Grace Fox
Published by Aspire Press
An imprint of Tyndale House Ministries
Carol Stream, Illinois
www.hendricksonrose.com

ISBN: 978-1-64938-051-7

Book design by Cristalle Kishi

Printed in the United States of America
011121VP

Contents

Dear Friend,

One minute we're basking in sunshine and the next—whoosh! A storm sweeps in and sends us scurrying for cover. Plans change in a heartbeat and force us to flex. Sometimes we accept the disruption with ease and grace. Other times, not so much.

Life's like that. Storms happen. It's not a matter of *if,* but *when* the wind and waves will batter our boat. Fear wants to grab us, but there's hope—God rules and we are safe in his grip. No matter what our storm looks like, we can be confident that he will carry us through it. His presence is with us and his Spirit empowers us. He repurposes our pain, using it for our good and for his glory.

I've written this little book to bring inner strength as you navigate the storm. May the words on these pages bring a blessing as you pause to reflect on the stories, ponder their application to your life, and make each sentence prayer your own.

Dear God, please infuse my friend with strength to navigate the storm. Grant reminders of your presence and assurance of your promises. Supply hope in abundance and faith to trust you in the details. I pray this in the power of your name with thanks in advance. Amen.

Know you are loved,

Grace Fox

God Prepares Us

What is mankind that you are mindful of them,
human beings that you care for them?

PSALM 8:4

Pause

My elderly mother's collapse and hospitalization signaled
the beginning of a storm season complicated by COVID
chaos. Not coincidentally, it blew in only three weeks after
I'd finished writing *Finding Hope in Crisis: Devotions for Calm
in Chaos*.

The writing process had immersed me in Scripture for hours
every day. It filled my mind with God's promises, truth, and
hope. I'd prayed over every detail of the project and for
the people in crises who would someday read it. Without
my realizing it, God was using my efforts to ready me for
the impending torrent.

Nothing fully prepares us for the storm when it strikes,
but our compassionate God often readies us in ways
unrecognizable at the time. He knows our future and the

challenges it will bring, and he's masterful at addressing them in advance. In hindsight, we can often identify certain circumstances as evidences of his grace and involvement in our lives. Nothing is happenstance. He orchestrates every detail of our lives, and that includes preparing us for the challenges ahead.

Ponder

How has God shown his care by preparing you for the storm you're experiencing?

Pray

God, help me recognize your involvement in my life and not credit it to mere coincidence.

"An important key to not becoming overwhelmed by what is going on around us is looking for evidences of God's hand at work in the midst of the turmoil and being simply overwhelmed with thankfulness to Him."

NANCY DEMOSS WOLGEMUTH,
Choosing Gratitude: Your Journey to Joy

Exhale

*Cast all your anxiety on him
because he cares for you.*

1 PETER 5:7

Pause

Both the sun and Sailor-Man (better known to most people as Gene, my husband) were still asleep when I rose to read my Bible and enjoy a cup of coffee with my Jesus. As always, our time together was precious. But on this occasion, I felt him nudge me to do something I hadn't done before.

"Exhale worry about your daughter's health." I took a deep breath and then let it out. It felt good. "Exhale worry about your friend's breast cancer diagnosis." Done. "Exhale worry about virus issues." Concern after concern came to mind without my searching for them. I hadn't realized worry's weight until it lifted, one exhale at a time.

Jesus commands us to cast our cares—the worries that weigh us down—on him. This means to hurl or forcefully heave them. Picture yourself throwing your anxieties, like a big burden, onto a pack mule's back. The animal is built to carry a load, and his labor spares us discomfort and pain.

Jesus' care for us runs deep; therefore, we can trust him with every detail of our lives. We can release our worries to him and breathe easy.

Ponder

List your worries and give them to Jesus, pausing to exhale between each one.

Pray

God, I'm carrying a weight too heavy for me. I give it now to you.

"Worst case scenarios will always exist in this life, but we don't have to give in to worrying about them. On occasion, sure, a few of them might happen to us but even then, as children of God, we can hold on to the truth that the best possible scenario is also true: God is with us. We are not alone. He is in control."

MARGARET FEINBERG, *Overcoming Worry: Finding Peace in the Midst of Uncertainty*

Tangled Threads

*Now we see things imperfectly, like puzzling
reflections in a mirror, but then we will see
everything with perfect clarity.*

1 CORINTHIANS 13:12 NLT

Pause

As newlyweds, my husband and I moved to Nepal where he worked as a civil engineer on a hydro-electric power project. For two years, I struggled with culture shock, isolation, language learning, and adjusting to life in a mud house with no electricity or running water. Some days, I wanted to catch the first flight back to the familiar, but I wanted to obey God's call on my life more.

Sailor-Man and I eventually decided to spend the rest of our lives in that land. A career mission agency interviewed us to join their staff, but a week later our second child was born with hydrocephalus (too much water on the brain). Medical needs forced an immediate return to North America. We've visited Nepal several times since, but living there again is improbable.

I look at that section of my life's tapestry and see only tangled threads. What was the point of our time in Nepal? I have no answer, but I believe God never makes mistakes. Every thread and knot serve a purpose as he weaves the tapestry of our lives. Someday we'll see the finished product and smile at its beauty.

Ponder

Describe the view of your current situation: tangled threads or beautiful tapestry?

Pray

God, grant peace, even when the tangled threads seem random and messy.

> "On earth, the underside of the tapestry was tangled and unclear; but in heaven, we will stand amazed to see the topside of the tapestry and how God beautifully embroidered each circumstance into a pattern for our good and His glory."

JONI EARECKSON TADA,
Heaven: Your Real Home

In the Right Place

The LORD directs the steps of the godly.
He delights in every detail of their lives.
Though they stumble, they will never fall,
for the LORD holds them by the hand.

PSALM 37:23–24 NLT

Pause

The Israelites followed God's instructions to camp by the Red Sea after leaving Egypt, but doing so left them in apparent peril. With water before them and the desert on both sides, they had no way to escape Pharaoh's approaching army. "Why did you bring us out here to die?" they asked Moses (Exodus 14:11, NLT).

We might feel the same way about our circumstances. We love God and follow his commands as best we know. We anticipate life going well, but then the opposite happens.

God always works according to plan. He led the Israelites to that campground because he wanted to do something extraordinary there (Exodus 14:4). He occasionally leads us to difficult places and situations for the same reason. He wants to reveal his power in ways not possible otherwise.

We might wonder whether God messed up, we misunderstood his lead, or we did something wrong. Rest assured; he makes no mistakes. He's up to something, and we are exactly where he wants us at this time.

Ponder

Why might God have brought you to this place at this time?

Pray

God, I don't understand what you're doing, but I trust you.

"So, take a deep breath and recall this deeper secret of the Christian life: when you are in a difficult place, realize that the Lord either placed you there or allowed you to be there, for reasons perhaps known for now only to Himself. The same God who led you in will lead you out."

ROBERT J. MORGAN, *The Red Sea Rules: The Same God Who Led You In Will Lead You Out*

Switchbacks

I know, LORD, that our lives are not our own.
We are not able to plan our own course.

JEREMIAH 10:23 NLT

Pause

Some mountains have switchback roads carved into them, resembling a giant zigzag. A vehicle driving on it goes one direction first, navigates a hairpin curve, and then goes the opposite direction. Repeat.

The description sounds much like life. We head in one direction but suddenly our circumstances change and send us in a different direction. We travel that route for a few months or years and then—bam! Another hairpin curve happens and off we go again.

Back and forth. Back and forth. Our journey zigs and zags in directions we would not necessarily choose for ourselves. Sometimes the new route leads us through quiet valleys that rest our souls. Other times it takes us along inclines that leave us white-knuckled and gasping for grace.

When the road suddenly takes a direction not in our plans, we needn't panic or wonder what went wrong. God is in control, and his intended journey for us is far better than the plans we make. We can trust him implicitly because of who he is—wise, loving, and faithful.

Ponder

Identify a switchback you've taken and where it led.

Pray

God, take the wheel and travel with me on the journey you've planned.

"Life is not a straight line leading from one blessing to the next and then finally to heaven. Life is a winding and troubled road. Switchback after switchback. And the point of biblical stories like Joseph and Job and Esther and Ruth is to help us feel in our bones (not just know in our heads) that God is for us in all these strange turns.... He is plotting the course and managing the troubles with far-reaching purposes for our good and for the glory of Jesus Christ."

JOHN PIPER, *A Sweet and Bitter Providence: Sex, Race, and the Sovereignty of God*

The Next Thing

I will instruct you and teach you in the way
you should go; I will counsel you
with my loving eye on you.

PSALM 32:8

Pause

Our eldest daughter was born with hydrocephalus when Sailor-Man and I lived in Nepal. Because she needed surgery to alleviate cranial pressure, an immediate return to the United States was in order. Sailor-Man did the trip with our baby, but my physical state made it impossible for me to go with them.

Our circumstances constituted a perfect storm: We had a critically ill baby in a neonatal intensive care unit but no health insurance. We needed a place to live, a car, and a job. Because I was Canadian, I had to begin immediate processing to become a legal resident alien. As if those concerns weren't enough, reverse culture shock hit us.

Our brains functioned as though in a fog, but God led us through it one step at a time. Focusing on one thing first, and then the next, and then the next, helped us survive as life settled into a new normal.

Our wise and faithful God will do the same for you, my friend. He will guide you through this experience. Don't try to see far into the future. Just do the next right thing.

Ponder

What is the next thing you should or could do now?

Pray

God, guide me through this day one step at a time.

> "Hope begins in the dark, the stubborn hope that if you just show up and try to do the right thing, the dawn will come. You wait and watch and work; you don't give up."
>
> ANNE LAMOTT,
> *Bird by Bird: Some Instructions on Writing and Life*

No Comparisons, Please

Since we are surrounded by such a great cloud of witnesses, let us throw off everything that hinders and the sin that so easily entangles. And let us run with perseverance the race marked out for us.

HEBREWS 12:1

Pause

I weathered a unique storm when Sailor-Man took our three-day-old daughter from Nepal to North America for life-saving surgery. Because I'd delivered her by cesarean section, international travel restrictions said I was not allowed to fly for two weeks. I said goodbye to my baby not knowing whether I'd see her alive again.

When I tell my story, someone invariably says, "I don't know how you survived that experience. I went through a hard time, too, but it was nowhere near as difficult as yours." Truth be told, I've done the same thing—fallen into the comparison trap—while listening to others' stories.

Comparing storms has no value. Everyone approaches challenges through a multi-faceted lens that includes personality, upbringing, background, beliefs, and resources available. A mountain to one might be a molehill to another, and comparison only leads to feelings of pride, envy, or inadequacy.

God has a plan and purpose for each of us. Our responsibility is to reckon with our own story in a healthy way, not to compare it with others.

Ponder

Identify a time when you compared your hardship with another's. What was the outcome?

Pray

God, help me handle my hardship in a healthy way.

"Comparing your trauma to someone else's is like trying to compare children. Everyone is different. Just because someone else's story seems more traumatic doesn't mean yours is not. Trauma is something to reckon with and it's okay to own your story."

MARY DEMUTH

Recognizing Jesus' Presence

*Early in the morning, Jesus stood on the shore,
but the disciples did not realize that it was Jesus.*

JOHN 21:4

Pause

The disciples fished all night but caught nothing. Exhausted and empty-handed, they turned their boat toward shore. A man called to them as they approached, "Friends, haven't you any fish?" (John 21:5).

Perhaps fatigue blurred the disciples' vision. Maybe trauma they'd experienced over Jesus' recent arrest and crucifixion clouded their thinking. For whatever reason, the fishermen did not recognize the man in their midst as their beloved Messiah.

The men's oversight did not offend Jesus. He knew their hearts, their deepest needs, and the great stress they'd been under. He responded by loving on them with a boatload of encouragement, home-cooked breakfast on the beach, and meaningful conversation.

We're not unlike the disciples. Challenging circumstances consume our time, energy, and attention. Exhaustion and stress can blur our spiritual vision and blind us to Jesus' presence. Thankfully, our accidental oversight doesn't diminish his love for us. He understands our deepest needs and offers encouragement when we need it most.

Ponder

Identify at least one way in which Jesus has shown up and offered unexpected encouragement.

Pray

God, please open my eyes to recognize your presence and activity in my circumstances.

"Through hundreds of ways, God whispers,
'I love you and I am always with you.'
Don't miss Him or His presence as you go through
this day. Open your eyes of faith and look for Him
in the most simple of ways. The experience can be
extraordinary and life-changing!"

RON LAMBROS,
*All My Love, Jesus: Personal Reminders
from the Heart of God*

Spiritual Perception

Many of the people who were with Mary believed in
Jesus when they saw this happen. But some went to the
Pharisees and told them what Jesus had done.

JOHN 11:45-46 NLT

Pause

Mourners placed Lazarus's body in the tomb four days before Jesus came to town. Imagine their shock and awe when Jesus called the dead man's name and he emerged walking unassisted, still wrapped in grave clothes.

Everyone on site witnessed the same scene but perceived it differently. Some onlookers rejoiced and believed in Jesus as the promised Messiah. Others refused to believe and tattled to the religious leaders who wanted to get rid of Jesus.

We, too, have our own perceptions about God, especially in the face of hardship. We either marvel at his wisdom, compassion, and sovereignty, or we question his character. Rather than rest in his control, we try to yank it from his hands.

We often develop perceptions about God based on upbringing and past experiences, but beware: human error leads to wrong conclusions. Perceiving correctly about who God is and what he's doing in and through our difficulty requires a knowledge of the truth.

Ponder

What truth about God's nature do you lean on most when you're hurting or anxious?

Pray

God, align my perception of you with the truth.

> "When Jesus raised Lazarus to life, the miracle was so spectacular many people believed in Jesus. However, some witnessed the same miracle and were motivated instead to betray Jesus (John 11:47–48). How could people witness such an event yet miss God's message? It was a matter of spiritual perception."
>
> HENRY BLACKABY AND RICHARD BLACKABY,
> *Hearing God's Voice*

A Bigger Plan

Now to him who is able to do immeasurably more
than all we ask or imagine, according to
his power that is at work within us.

EPHESIANS 3:20

Pause

Why doesn't God answer my prayers? Nancy wondered. Doctors had said she needed a heart valve replaced, but the thought of surgery terrified her. She'd relentlessly asked God to heal her, but her prayers seemed to fall on deaf ears.

Nancy found the answer after the inevitable turned urgent. While in recovery on the cardiac ward, she engaged in conversation with a hospital supervisor. Their chat turned to spiritual matters, and Nancy told the woman about Christ's love. Seeing her visible response helped Nancy understand that her heart surgery was part of a bigger plan. God said no to a miraculous healing because he was preparing the supervisor to hear and receive the gospel.

We, too, might sometimes wonder why God isn't answering our prayers. It's possible that our asking is amiss, but it's also possible that he's working behind the scenes on a plan only he understands. Our circumstances play a role, and we can trust him to bring every detail together to accomplish his purposes in his time.

Ponder

For what have you relentlessly asked God but have not seen a visible answer?

Pray

God, I don't understand why you seem silent, but I choose to trust your plan.

"We might not see God answering our prayers as we wish, but that doesn't mean he isn't working on them."

NANCY SABATO,
The Call with Nancy Sabato (podcast)

Bringing Thoughts Captive

We demolish arguments and every pretension that sets itself up against the knowledge of God, and we take captive every thought to make it obedient to Christ.

2 CORINTHIANS 10:5

Pause

During the pandemic, my 88-year-old mom spent several weeks in the hospital after she collapsed in her home. From there she was moved to a sub-acute care unit for further recovery. Medical professionals assessed her needs and called a family meeting. They said independent living was not an option, and they explained the process for finding an appropriate permanent assisted-living facility.

Some parts of the process made sense. Others seemed unrealistic, even unkind. I left the meeting discouraged. What did my mother's future hold? My thoughts raced toward a dark and fear-filled place where what-if questions ran rampant.

I've written a book and Bible study about moving from fear to freedom. I speak on this topic at women's events. Now I had to intentionally practice what I preach. I admitted my fears to God, asked him to help me reel them in, and then focused on his promises to care for our needs. Doing so brought fear under control, allowed me to think rationally, and drew me into a place of peace.

Ponder

Identify thoughts that are running rampant and causing fear in you.

Pray

God, reel in my fearful thoughts and bring them under your control.

"When we begin to think about our thoughts, perhaps for the first time, we can stop the downward spiral. We can reset and redirect them. That's our hope. Not that we would wrestle each and every fear, but that we would allow God to take up so much space in our thinking that our fears will shrink in comparison."

JENNIE ALLEN, *Get out of Your Head: Stopping the Spiral of Toxic Thoughts*

Why Are You Crying?

"Dear woman, why are you crying?" the angels asked her.
"Because they have taken away my Lord," she replied,
"and I don't know where they have put him."

JOHN 20:13 NLT

Pause

Mary stood outside Jesus' empty tomb and wept. *Who stole my Lord? she wondered. And where did they take him?*

Suddenly, angels interrupted Mary's musings with a question of their own: "Why are you crying?" The query was not meant as a reprimand. They asked it with respect and concern, and they prefaced it with love: "Dear woman." Jesus appeared moments later, offered the same greeting, and asked the same question.

Repetition in Scripture signals importance. No doubt Jesus and the angels spoke these words to acknowledge Mary's pain in her distress. But perhaps they also meant to help her identify inaccurate assumptions about her situation. Believing someone had stolen Jesus' body had caused undue sorrow. Hearing and answering the question paved the way for truth to be revealed. Despair turned to hope when she realized she'd jumped to a wrong conclusion.

When we're in a place of distress, we find clarity by personalizing the same question: "Why am I crying?" Try it. The answer might surprise you.

Ponder

Are you carrying unnecessary stress from an inaccurate assumption? If so, what is it?

Pray

God, change my wrong assumptions to a right understanding.

"A person is the product of his thoughts.
I want to be happy and hopeful. Therefore, I will
have thoughts that are happy and hopeful.
I refuse to be victimized by my circumstances."

MAX LUCADO,
*On the Anvil: Stories on Being
Shaped into God's Image*

No Directions Needed

Trust in the lord with all your heart;
do not depend on your own understanding.

PROVERBS 3:5 NLT

Pause

Being directionally challenged isn't easy. I'm the only person I know who gets lost in a cul-de-sac. I'm also mathematically challenged. I'm a words girl, so I'm beyond grateful that Sailor-Man understands numbers. And then there's computer technology and social media. I've yet to see anyone knock down my door, asking for help.

My understanding is limited. I shouldn't be surprised, then, by a recent aha moment about my prayer life. "You don't have to give me directions," the Holy Spirit whispered one day. That's when I realized my prayers in life's hard places usually sound like this: "God, do such-and-such to fix it." Imagine me—a woman who gets lost using a GPS and who can't balance a checkbook—telling God what to do. Silly, right?

Our wisdom, knowledge, and understanding fall exponentially short of God's. He knows everything about our circumstances from beginning to end. He invites us to talk with him about them, but he doesn't need us to tell him what to do. He's got this, and we can trust him.

Ponder

What's one question for which you have no answer within the context of your current challenge?

Pray

God, thank you for not expecting me to give you the answers.

"Prayer is not telling God what to do. Prayer is partnering with God to see that His will is done. You don't have to fully understand what God's will is in order to pray that His will be done."

STORMIE OMARTIAN,
The Power of Praying for Your Adult Children

Peace Be Still

*[Jesus] awoke and rebuked the wind and said
to the sea, "Peace! Be still!" And the wind ceased,
and there was a great calm.*

MARK 4:39 ESV

Pause

The disciples were in a boat … in a windstorm … in the dark. And the boat was nearly swamped. It couldn't get much worse. The one whose idea it was to set sail was sleeping in the stern, so the disciples woke him with accusatory shouts of "Teacher, don't you care if we drown?" (Mark 4:38)

Jesus didn't try to settle their nerves with a sermonette about trust. Instead, he spoke three well-chosen words: "Peace! Be still!" Do you suppose he meant those words not only for the storm but for the sailors, too?

Think about it: Jesus had assured a safe arrival when he said, "Let us go over to the other side" (Mark 4:35). He modeled freedom from fear when he slept. He was God-in-flesh, creator of heaven and earth, his identity guaranteed control over the weather.

With Jesus in the boat, the disciples had every reason to experience peace rather than panic. So do we because Jesus is with us. When fear rises, let's borrow his words and speak them to ourselves: "Peace! Be still."

Ponder

Name the fear that steals your peace.

Pray

God, I long for peace but I long for you, the peace-giver, more.

"When we talk about the peace of God, don't think of singing and swaying and holding hands in a circle. The peace of God is strong, intense, palpable, real. You can sense its stable presence giving you inner security despite insecure circumstances."

PRISCILLA SHIRER,
Discerning the Voice of God:
How to Recognize When He Speaks

Pursued by Goodness

*Surely your goodness and unfailing love will
pursue me all the days of my life, and I will live
in the house of the Lord forever.*

PSALM 23:6 NLT

Pause

I recently visited a couple who have a preschool-age son. Everywhere Daddy went, the boy went, too. He tagged along to the hardware store. He followed his father downstairs to the workbench. He shadowed him in the backyard, watching him cultivate a garden plot. A ladybug distracted him momentarily, and then the neighbor's cat, but sooner or later he remembered his original mission and rejoined his dad.

The scene reminded me of Psalm 23:6. You and I are being followed too—by God's goodness and unfailing love. But this is more than a mere tagging along or shadowing. This is an intentional, hot pursuit.

God's goodness and unfailing love are near every day, even on the difficult ones and those we'd like to forget.

We might not be aware of them, but they've got us in their sight and they'll keep us there until the day we move from earth to heaven. They're faithful companions everywhere we go, and nothing distracts them for an instant. We are their focus, and they are our friends forever.

Ponder

What's one recent evidence of God's goodness to you?

Pray

God, I'm grateful that I can never outrun your love.

"If God does what you think he should do, trust him. If God doesn't do what you think he should do, trust him. If you pray and believe God for a miracle and he does it, trust him. If your worst nightmare comes true, believe he is sovereign. Believe he is good."

CRAIG GROESCHEL,
The Christian Atheist: Believing in God but Living As If He Doesn't Exist

Heart Health Matters

May these words of my mouth and this
meditation of my heart be pleasing in your sight,
LORD, my Rock and my Redeemer.

PSALM 19:14

Pause

The words we speak under pressure are often telltale signs of heart trouble. Do we complain about our hardship or blame others for it? Express all-consuming fear about the outcome? Rehearse all the negative possibilities? If so, we've developed a case of wrong beliefs.

Believing God is distant and disinterested in our plight leaves us feeling lonely and helpless. Thinking he is harsh and unkind leaves us feeling unloved. Assuming he is not big enough to make a way through our circumstances leaves us feeling weak and hopeless.

The words we speak reveal an underlying problem. The cure is to align our beliefs about God with the truth: He is near and cares about our concerns (1 Peter 5:7). He is good at all times (Psalm 34:8). He is strong enough and able to make a way, even though there seems to be no way (Proverbs 3:5–6).

How can we know when our heart is healthy? The words we speak to ourselves and to others will reflect hope.

Ponder

What do the words you speak under pressure say about your heart health?

Pray

God, align my heart with the truth about who you are, so my words reflect hope.

"Imagine how differently you might
approach each day by simply stating:
God is good.
God is good to me.
God is good at being God.
And today is yet another page
in our great love story.
Nothing that happens to you today will change that
or even alter it in the slightest way."

LYSA TERKEURST, *Uninvited: Living Loved
When You Feel Less Than, Left Out, and Lonely*

Answer the Question

"Be strong and courageous! Don't be afraid or discouraged
because of the king of Assyria or his mighty army,
for there is a power far greater on our side! ...
We have the LORD our God to help us
and to fight our battles for us!"
Hezekiah's words greatly encouraged the people.

2 CHRONICLES 32:7–8 NLT

Pause

King Hezekiah prepared to defend Jerusalem from Assyria's
attack. Then he called his people together and told them
to not be afraid because God was on their side.

The Assyrian king and his officials mocked God and scoffed
at Jerusalem's dependence on him. "What makes you
think your God can rescue you from me?" the king asked
(2 Chronicles 32:14 NLT). He didn't pose the question for
conversation's sake. He used it as a ploy to plant seeds of
doubt about God's ability to save his people.

In the midst of a storm, the enemy of our soul whispers,
"What makes you think your God can rescue you?" He

uses this tactic to instill doubt and fear, but let's resist his strategy. Recall the truth about God and stand firm. He is a power far greater than any problem we face, and he loves us enough to fight on our behalf.

Ponder

What makes you think your God can rescue you?

Pray

God, I don't think you can rescue me. I *know* you can!

"Trust God. Believe with every fiber of your being that He will faithfully fulfill His promises. Do not just say, 'I hope the Lord will come to my aid.' Do not merely stop at declaring, 'I know He can work everything out.' Exhibit the highest level of faith by proclaiming, 'I am absolutely certain my heavenly Father will help me—it's as good as done.'"

CHARLES F. STANLEY,
Every Day in His Presence

Bring It On

Yes, everything else is worthless when compared with the infinite value of knowing Christ Jesus my Lord.

PHILIPPIANS 3:8 NLT

Pause

I've followed Christ long enough to know that praying "Lord, teach me to know you more intimately" is an open invitation to adversity. It's like saying, "Bring it on!"

Knowing Christ more deeply became my heart's cry in 2017. God answered by telling us to purge our earthly possessions and move aboard a sailboat full-time. It sounds romantic and exciting, I know, but not so much when the diesel furnace dies in dead winter or when the freezer goes kaput and its contents thaws. Not so much when the dock turns icy and sends you sprawling face first, or when you have to carry the laundry a city block in the pouring rain. Not so much when the kids and grandkids can't visit at the same time because space is too limited.

The transition from shore to boat stripped away everything I held dear and taught me a lesson that money can't buy: Jesus is enough. I used to teach this truth, but now I believe it. Adversity made it a blessed reality in my life, and I wouldn't trade it for anything.

Ponder

What spiritual reality has come alive for you through adversity?

Pray

God, bring it on. Use adversity to teach me spiritual realities that money can't buy.

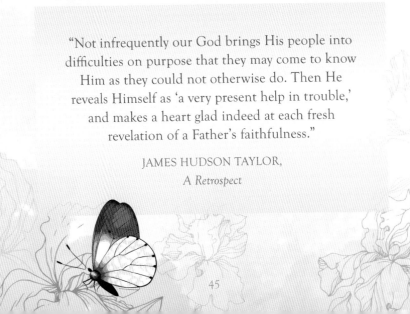

"Not infrequently our God brings His people into difficulties on purpose that they may come to know Him as they could not otherwise do. Then He reveals Himself as 'a very present help in trouble,' and makes a heart glad indeed at each fresh revelation of a Father's faithfulness."

JAMES HUDSON TAYLOR,
A Retrospect

Vulnerable

After fasting forty days and forty nights,
[Jesus] was hungry. The tempter came to him
and said, "If you are the Son of God,
tell these stones to become bread."

MATTHEW 4:2–3

Pause

Jesus was in a vulnerable place when he finished his forty-day fast, and sure enough, that's when Satan showed up. Knowing Jesus was hungry, he aimed a fiery arrow at his appetite. His attack failed because Jesus knew better than to let his emotions dictate his response.

We fall into a vulnerable place when we're battle weary. Satan always knows when to show up, and he shoots at our weak spot. When we're overtired, scared, or discouraged, he lures us to say something regrettable or do something foolish.

The enemy wins if we let our emotions control us, but his fiery arrows bounce off our backs when we stand on truth as Jesus did. Jesus didn't argue or try to reason with the devil. He simply fired back with truth: "It is written: 'Man shall not live on bread alone, but on every word that comes from the mouth of God'" (Matthew 4:4).

We may be vulnerable, but we don't have to succumb to temptation. Jesus showed us how to do it.

Ponder

What temptations do you face in your vulnerable place?

Pray

God, give me the desire and the power to say no to the devil.

"We are not responsible for the circumstances we are in, but we are responsible for the way we allow those circumstances to affect us; we can either allow them to get on top of us or we can allow them to transform us into what God wants us to be."

OSWALD CHAMBERS,
Conformed to His Image/The Servant as His Lord: Lessons on Living like Jesus

El-Shaddai

When Abram was ninety-nine years old,
*the L*ORD *appeared to him and said,*
"I am El-Shaddai–'God Almighty.'
Serve me faithfully and live a blameless life."

GENESIS 17:1 NLT

Pause

God helps us understand his character through his names. "God Almighty" comes from the Hebrew *El-Shaddai. El* speaks of God's strength and prominence. *Shaddai* describes him as the one who completely satisfies. He is all-sufficient. Better yet—he's more than enough.

God first introduced himself as El-Shaddai when he promised to make ninety-nine-year-old Abram into a mighty nation (Genesis 17:1, 4 NLT). Nothing short of a miracle would see Abram and his barren, post-menopausal wife conceive a son from whom would come countless descendants. El-Shaddai—all-powerful and more than enough to conquer the impossible—performed that miracle.

Do you need a miracle today? Call on the name of El-Shaddai—God Almighty. He introduced himself using this name to strengthen our faith when we feel weak. Because of who he is, nothing stops him from fulfilling his purposes for our lives. He is more than able to supply our needs, no matter what they are. He is more than able to do the impossible.

Ponder

For what need are you trusting El-Shaddai's sufficiency?

Pray

God, help me live by faith in your sufficiency rather than in fear over my insufficiencies.

"Faith is not believing in my own unshakable belief.
Faith is believing an unshakable God
when everything in me trembles and quakes."

BETH MOORE,
*Praying God's Word: Breaking Free
from Spiritual Strongholds*

Repurposed

We can rejoice, too, when we run into problems and trials,
for we know that they help us develop endurance.
And endurance develops strength of character, and
character strengthens our confident hope of salvation.

ROMANS 5:3–4 NLT

Pause

Dealing with five-year-old Austin's obsessive-compulsive-disorder nearly drove Michelle to the brink one night. Feeling like a failure as a mother and blaming herself for his diagnosis, she decided to run away. When she turned the key in her van's ignition, however, music from a Christian radio station blared. One song after another reminded her that God loved her, knew her needs, and was in control.

That evening, Michelle realized that God wanted to repurpose her experience, as hard as it was, for a greater good. She began looking for ways in which he was doing this. She saw her family grow closer to God by praying together about Austin's anxiety. She learned to draw from the Lord's strength, and she developed empathy for other parents at their wits' end, which in turn opened doors to provide encouragement.

Michelle discovered a hidden jewel in crisis: be aware that God is up to something good in the midst of hardship. There's a reason for his allowing it in your life.

Ponder

Identify one good thing God has done as a result of your situation.

Pray

God, repurpose my pain for your perfect pleasure.

"Because I've seen God work through my own past struggles, I've begun to seek him and look for his repurposing when I'm still in the middle of a new adversity rather than after it passes. It gives me a greater sense of peace about my worries when I know my God is working it all out for my good and his glory."

MICHELLE RAYBURN,
The Repurposed and Upcycled Life:
When God Turns Trash to Treasure

Why Are You So Afraid?

The disciples went and woke [Jesus], saying,
"Lord, save us! We're going to drown!" He replied,
"You of little faith, why are you so afraid?"
Then he got up and rebuked the winds and the waves,
and it was completely calm.

MATTHEW 8:25–26

Pause

I grew up in a landlubber family on the Alberta prairies. Sailor-Man grew up in a family that lived on waterfront property and enjoyed boating. Our dissimilar backgrounds explain our different responses when sailing in choppy seas.

I scream and pray a lot. Sailor-Man, while respectful of my jitters, catches the wind so our vessel can do what it was built to do. Beyond a doubt, he's more relaxed than me because he knows boats and understands the science behind sailing.

I empathize with the disciples' fear in the storm. It terrified them, but howling wind, choppy waves, and boating buddies didn't stop Jesus from sleeping. He was more relaxed than the others because he knew who he was— the one who created and controlled the weather. The disciples were not yet convinced.

Knowing Jesus intimately is the key to releasing our fear and learning to rest in the storm. We might say it works like this: Know Jesus. No fear.

Ponder

Answer Jesus' question: "Why are you so afraid?"

Pray

God, teach me to know you intimately so I can rest rather than stress in the storm.

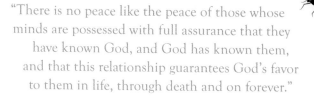

"There is no peace like the peace of those whose minds are possessed with full assurance that they have known God, and God has known them, and that this relationship guarantees God's favor to them in life, through death and on forever."

J. I. PACKER, *Knowing God*

Valuable

God paid a high price for you,
so don't be enslaved by the world.

1 CORINTHIANS 7:23 NLT

Pause

Hosting one-night women's events with free admission led to a fascinating discovery: many women reserved seats in advance but then failed to attend. Advisors said, "They'll come if you charge five dollars." Their suggestion worked. Apparently, people place value on goods and services for which they pay, even if it's only a few dollars.

When we land in a hard place, Satan tells us that God doesn't really love or value us. If he did, these things wouldn't be happening, right? Wrong.

God paid the highest price possible to redeem me and you from the slavery of sin. This speaks volumes about the degree to which he values us. We cannot comprehend our worth to him, but we can be certain that he will do everything in his power to ensure our well-being. He has our best interest in mind at all times. We are his precious and beloved children, bought with the blood of his son, and we matter deeply to him (1 John 3:1; John 3:16).

Ponder

Compare the care you bestow on something that cost you dearly versus something that cost little or nothing.

Pray

God, help me value the price you paid for me as much as you value me.

"Even though I only just found out that I was adopted, God has always known, and he has always loved me. And since *that* has never changed, therefore essentially *nothing* has changed. I may not be who I thought I was, but I still am who he says I am. And I am more. I am loved. I am his."

CHRISTINE CAINE,
Undaunted: Daring to Do What God Calls You to Do

God's Promises
Bring Hope

When neither sun nor stars appeared
for many days and the storm continued raging,
we finally gave up all hope of being saved.

ACTS 27:20

Pause

Imagine 276 people on board an ancient Egyptian sailing ship battered for many days by hurricane-force winds. Imagine the fear and desperation, the physical exhaustion and mental stress, and the stench. Paul was aboard this vessel, and he wrote that the passengers gave up all hope for rescue. Is it any wonder?

But God knew of Paul's peril and sent a promise through an angel. He said, "Do not be afraid, Paul. You must stand trial before Caesar; and God has graciously given you the lives of all who sail with you" (Acts 27:24).

Paul took God at his word. He told his fellow passengers, "So keep up your courage, men, for I have faith in God that it will happen just as he told me" (Acts 27:25).

Clinging to God's promises is all we can muster on some days, but that's enough to bolster our courage. Holding on to faith in our faithful God, as Paul did, will see us through.

Ponder

Finish this sentence: I will keep up my courage because

_____.

Pray

God, keep up my courage as I keep your promises in mind.

"You must stay upon the Lord; and come what may—winds, waves, cross-seas, thunder, lightning, frowning rocks, roaring breakers—no matter what, you must lash yourself to the helm, and hold fast your confidence in God's faithfulness, His covenant engagement, His everlasting love in Christ Jesus."

RICHARD FULLER

Pray and Listen

Fearing that we would be dashed against the rocks,
[the sailors] dropped four anchors from the stern
and prayed for daylight.

ACTS 27:29-30

Pause

The sailors aboard the doomed Egyptian vessel were beyond exhausted and scared. The storm at sea had caused havoc for fourteen days and nights, and now their vessel approached a rocky shoreline in the dark. Panicked, the men cried to their gods for help. And then what did they do? They took matters into their own hands. Paul wrote, "In an attempt to escape from the ship, the sailors let the lifeboat down into the sea, pretending they were going to lower some anchors from the bow" (Acts 27:30).

We, too, pray for help in desperate times, but hopefully we don't try to rush to our own rescue. Prayer is more than telling God our needs. It's also listening for his response. He might tell us to take specific action, or he might tell us to wait for him to act. Let's resist the temptation to run ahead of him by taking matters into our own hands lest we create chaos for ourselves and others. Let's pray and listen and then respond accordingly.

Ponder

Am I willing to listen for God's response to my prayers and then obey him?

Pray

God, you hear my prayers. Help me hear and obey you.

"While walking through a dark season, if we attempt to navigate our lives by what we feel, we will run aground onto the rocks. We must navigate by what we know is true no matter what we feel."

SHEILA WALSH,
The Storm Inside: Trade the Chaos of How You Feel for the Truth of Who You Are

In His Sight

But the eyes of the LORD are on those who
fear him, on those whose hope is in his
unfailing love, to deliver them from death
and keep them alive in famine.

PSALM 33:18–19

Pause

Sailor-Man and I recently spent time with five of our youngest grandchildren at a playground. With a dozen other kids running around the same space, we found that keeping our kiddos in sight at all times was a full-time job. My heart fluttered a few times when I thought I'd lost one.

I love my grandchildren to the moon and back, but God loves his kids even more. No matter where we are, he has us in sight. Some folks interpret this to mean he constantly watches us to catch us doing wrong, but that's not the case. He keeps his eyes on us to deliver us from trouble. He knows when we fall, when we hurt, and when we cry. He sees us when we feel lonely, afraid, bewildered, or desperate. He never sleeps or becomes distracted;

therefore, he never loses track of where we are or how we're doing.

We're in God's sight, and there's no better place to be.

Ponder

What does God see when he looks at you today?

Pray

God, thank you for the peace that comes from knowing you're watching me.

"Someone is watching you right now as you read this. Think about that. The God who loans you life sees your every move, hears each word you speak, and knows your every thought. And this is a good thing. You are seen by God. Noticed. *Known.*"

FRANCIS CHAN AND LISA CHAN,
You and Me Forever: Marriage in Light of Eternity

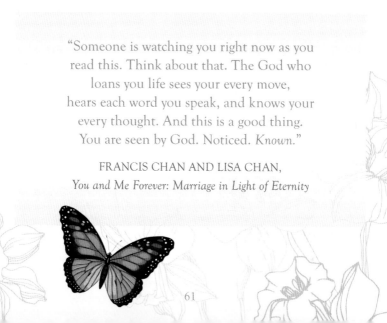

Disappointment

Consider it pure joy, my brothers and sisters, whenever you
face trials of many kinds, because you know that the
testing of your faith produces perseverance.
Let perseverance finish its work so that you may
be mature and complete, not lacking anything.

JAMES 1:2-4

Pause

The pandemic brought a plethora of disappointments.
It limited family get-togethers, weddings, funerals, and
graduations. It stopped travel, closed businesses, and
canceled church services. It upended normal and left us
wondering what a new normal might look like.

There's no denying it: disappointment hurts. We can either
hang on to the pain and become bitter or allow God
to use it for good and become better. Doing the latter
turns our disappointment into a character development
program of sorts.

When we let him, God uses disappointments to instill in us
qualities including patience, contentment, and gratitude.

Through them, he can deepen our prayer life and create greater empathy for others who are also experiencing broken dreams and dashed expectations.

Disappointment hurts, but dealing with it well yields results. We grow personally and spiritually when we let God use it for our good and his glory.

Ponder

Identify at least one good thing that's come through a disappointment in your life.

Pray

God, take my pain of disappointment and use it for your highest purposes.

"The disappointment has come ... not because God desires to hurt you or make you miserable or to demoralize you or ruin your life or keep you from ever knowing happiness ... He wants you to be perfect and complete in every aspect, lacking nothing ... *It's not the easy times that make you more like Jesus, but the hard times.*"

KAY ARTHUR, *As Silver Refined: Learning to Embrace Life's Disappointments*

Worship Songs

I will sing of your strength, in the morning
I will sing of your love; for you are my fortress,
my refuge in times of trouble.

PSALM 59:16

Pause

Worship music ministers deeply to my soul, especially when I'm grieving. So when, in the wake of a friend's betrayal, I stumbled across the song "All Is Well" by Robin Mark, I played it not once but multiple times in quick succession. I listened, cried, and when I was able, sang through my sobs.

The lyrics echoed my thoughts: I had no clue what God's plan was for me in this hurtful situation, but I could declare that all was well with my soul because my life was hidden in his hands.

I wish I could say that singing truth led to this relationship's complete restoration. Unfortunately, that's not the case. It did, however, help restore my soul. The lyrics turned my focus from my heartache to God's heart for me, his hurting child. The words assured me that he would never betray me and never stop loving me. I'd known those truths all along, but declaring them through song connected mind and emotions and took my understanding of them to a new level.

Ponder

What truths about God does your favorite worship song declare?

Pray

God, be the song in my heart when life hurts.

"I repeat the phrase *Christ my Comforter, Christ my Comforter*, as a prayer, as a way of asking for help and believing that help does exist. I don't know where the phrase even came from, but to me it's like music, like an incantation, something tattooed on my heart. *Christ my Comforter, Christ my Comforter*."

SHAUNA NIEQUIST,
Bittersweet: Thoughts on Change, Grace, and Learning the Hard Way

Never Too Busy

Then the woman, seeing that she could not go unnoticed, came trembling and fell at [Jesus'] feet. In the presence of all the people, she told why she had touched him and how she had been instantly healed.

LUKE 8:47

Pause

Jesus was en route to a twelve-year-old girl nearing death when a woman who'd exhausted medical options touched the hem of his garment in hopes of finding healing. Jesus stopped, turned his attention to her, and invited her to engage with him. Then he blessed her within earshot of the crowds who considered her untouchable. "Daughter, your faith has healed you. Go in peace" (Luke 8:48).

Jesus was a busy man but never too busy to extend grace. He did not view the woman as an interruption of a more important mission. Rather, he gave her his undivided attention, regarded her as precious, and blessed her with shalom—peace.

We might sometimes feel as though Jesus is too busy to care about our concerns. Maybe he thinks they're trivial. Maybe he thinks, *You again?*

Put those fears to rest, my friend. You matter to Jesus, and he's never too busy to give you his attention and have a conversation with you.

Ponder

What would you say to Jesus right now if he gave you his undivided attention?

Pray

God, help me never live too busy for you.

"This father always relates to his children in perfect love. This father is never absent. He is never disinterested. He is never preoccupied. He is never unable to respond to a need."

HENRY BLACKABY AND RICHARD BLACKABY,
Hearing God's Voice

Our Hope-Anchor

*We have this hope as an anchor
for the soul, firm and secure.*

HEBREWS 6:19

Pause

Sailor-Man and I enjoy boating to picturesque coves on British Columbia's coast. The first thing we do when we arrive at our destination, even before turning off the engine, is set the anchor into the sea bottom. Without the anchor set, our boat would drift.

We put significant trust in the anchor. Knowing it's in place enables us to tend to chores or relax. Properly set, it enables us to sleep at night without having to take turns keeping watch for safety's sake. It prevents wind and currents from pushing us into another boat or worse, onto shore. It's vital to our well-being, and we wouldn't dream of boating without it.

Scripture likens our hope in Christ and his promises to an anchor that holds our soul steadfast. It keeps us from drifting into despair when circumstances rock our boat. Placing our trust in anything less could be compared to setting our physical boat anchor on something that will not safely hold us, like seaweed. It guarantees disappoint, but faith in Christ and his promises keeps us secure. It's vital to our well-being and seriously, we can't do life without it.

Ponder

What promise from God's Word anchors your soul?

Pray

God, you are my anchor and I put my trust in you.

"In order to realize the worth of the anchor
we need to feel the stress of the storm."

CORRIE TEN BOOM,
Jesus Is Victor

When Giving Thanks Hurts

*I will offer to you the sacrifice of thanksgiving
and call on the name of the LORD.*

PSALM 116:17 ESV

Pause

In the Old Testament, God commanded the Israelites to offer animal sacrifices as worship. Only the finest critters would do. Those with a blemish or defect were considered unacceptable.

Suppose those animals could net a decent price in the market. How do you think their owners felt about sacrificing both animal and profit? Some may have wrestled with that, but they followed through in obedience toward holy God and gave him their best, even though it cost them.

The sacrifice of thanksgiving costs something, too. This is the response we give to the Lord even as the storm winds batter us. Accusing him of being unfair and doubting his sovereignty would be like giving him a defective or blemished offering. He deserves better. We might wrestle with expressing thankfulness when our heart hurts, but he deserves words of gratitude for his unending love and ability to turn broken into beautiful. We give thanks as an act of worship, even when it hurts, because God deserves our finest.

Ponder

What does your sacrifice of thanksgiving look like?

Pray

God, teach me to offer a thanksgiving sacrifice with joy in response to your love for me.

"My father always told us that if we will let God, He can use even our disappointments, even our annoyances to bring us a blessing. There's a practical way to start the process too: by thanking Him for whatever happens, no matter how disagreeable it seems."

CATHERINE MARSHALL,
Christy

Jesus Heals

*[The LORD] heals the brokenhearted
and binds up their wounds.*

PSALM 147:3

Pause

It wasn't supposed to be this way, thought Catherine when, after twelve years of marriage, her husband left her for another woman. *Divorce and single parenting weren't in my plan.* The betrayal devastated her and their four children. Living in a small town where everyone knew everyone's business made matters worse. So did the other woman's harassing letters and phone calls. Feelings of rejection and doubts about life being worthwhile pummeled her hope and self-confidence. She went through phases of denial, anger, and grief; and she dropped forty-five pounds without trying.

Friends' encouragement and her mother's wisdom played a role in Catherine's recovery. "Jesus experienced rejection, too," her mom said. "He knows how you feel." Catherine discovered those words to be true. As she sought to know Jesus more intimately, she experienced his love, support, and strength to rebuild her life one day at a time.

Life rarely turns out the way we plan. Broken and wounded for us, Jesus feels our pain and hurts with us. But he doesn't stop there. He restores our hope, renews our strength, and rebuilds shattered dreams. He promises to heal our hurting hearts, and he never betrays his word.

Ponder

What part of your heart feels broken?

Pray

God, my heart hurts. It needs the touch of your healing hand.

"I have become convinced that God thoroughly enjoys fixing and saving things that are broken. That means that no matter how hurt and defeated you feel, no matter how badly you have been damaged, God can repair you. God can give anyone a second chance."

MELODY CARLSON,
Damaged: A Violated Trust

Teach Me to Pray

One day Jesus was praying in a certain place.
When he finished, one of his disciples said
to him, "Lord, teach us to pray,
just as John taught his disciples."

LUKE 11:1

Pause

Sudden tension in a family relationship hurt deeply. In desperation, I resorted to telling God what to do: "I need you to convict and change that person. I need you to make this strife go away." Nothing happened prayer-wise, but my burden grew heavier by the day. Everything changed the morning I stopped bossing God.

"Father, teach me how to pray in this situation," I said, looking at a canvas print of my extended family. This thought instantly came to mind: "With our hearts as your canvas, paint what you want our family relationships to look like." A half dozen insights about God's role as master artist followed. Each reassured me that he would heal the hurt in his time and way. I was to trust him, practice patience, and accept the outcome. My burden lifted, and peace took its place.

Are you like me—telling God how to fix your circumstances? It's time to let him be the boss. Ask him to teach you how to pray.

$\mathcal{P}onder$

Are you bossing God through prayer or letting him be the boss?

$\mathcal{P}ray$

God, you are all-wise. Please show me how to pray in this situation.

"The prayer we know as 'The Lord's Prayer' came from the Lord Jesus in direct response to His disciples' request: 'Lord, teach us to pray.' It has always fascinated me that they never asked Jesus to teach them to preach. They never asked Him to teach them to give or to witness. Perhaps, like us, the disciples were often at a loss when it came to communicating with the Almighty."

DAVID JEREMIAH, *Prayer, the Great Adventure*

Forging Friendship

Though the Lord gave you adversity for food and
suffering for drink, he will still be with you to teach you.
You will see your teacher with your own eyes.
Your own ears will hear him. Right behind you
a voice will say, "This is the way you should go,"
whether to the right or to the left.

ISAIAH 30:20–21 NLT

Pause

Samantha and I enjoyed a heart connection, but adversity forged our friendship. When her husband abandoned the family, she and I talked, cried, and prayed together on numerous occasions. Grief glued us together. Three decades later, we still treasure our relationship.

Walking through a storm hand-in-hand deepens relationship between those who share the pain. This proves true both with flesh-and-blood friendships and with God.

Crying to God in desperation makes us more attuned to hear his voice. Seeking his presence in our circumstances opens our eyes to see evidence of his love. Spiritual concepts we've known for years suddenly come alive. Bible promises assume new meaning.

Our human nature wants to avoid pain at all cost. But let's not wish it away too fast. Remember that God walks through the storms with us, and it's there—in the midst of our pain—that intimate friendship is forged.

Ponder

How is your storm forging friendship with God?

Pray

God, I want to know you as my best friend—my forever friend.

"God allows you to struggle, even though his power could prevent it, because his wise and compassionate authority knows that the benefit of your struggle far outweighs the comfort you may experience from his rescue."

JENNIFER ROTHSCHILD,
Life Is Just Not Fair: Finding Hope When Life Doesn't Make Sense

Wholly Reliable

The LORD's promises are pure, like silver refined
in a furnace, purified seven times over.

PSALM 12:6 NLT

Pause

As I sat vigil at my mother's bedside for nearly a week, a
new appreciation for God's promises was birthed in me.
Psalm 23:4 rose to the top: "Even though I walk through the
valley of the shadow of death, I will fear no evil, for you are
with me; your rod and your staff, they comfort me" (ESV).

I'd memorized these words as a child and could still recite
them, but Mom's final week allowed me to experience
them. The sense of God's presence in her hospital room
filled me with inexplicable peace and removed all fear
of the unknowns involved in saying farewell. I grieved, but
deep in my heart, I knew God was present and was helping
Mom transition to her heavenly home. He would also help
her loved ones left behind transition into life without her.

God's promises are flawless because he is holy. They're
steadfast because he never changes. They're true

because he cannot lie. They provide hope and an anchor for our soul. They're everything we need to walk unafraid in the valley of shadows.

Ponder

Fill in the blank to personalize Psalm 23:4: "Even though I walk through _____, I will fear no evil."

Pray

God, bring your promises to life in me.

"With the help of the Lord, you can handle life's challenges and heartaches, even the valley of the shadow of death. What comfort your fainting heart has, knowing that in those stumbling times of discouragement and despair, of depletion and seeming defeat, the Shepherd will find you ... restore and 'fix' you ... and follow you ... until you are well on your way again!"

ELIZABETH GEORGE,
Quiet Confidence for a Woman's Heart:
The Power of God's Restoration and Healing

God in the Darkness

Do not gloat over me, my enemy!
Though I have fallen, I will rise.
Though I sit in darkness,
the LORD will be my light.

MICAH 7:8

Pause

Sarah's life looked like a dream come true, but depression threatened to shatter it. A belief she'd embraced from childhood intensified her struggle: God is "the light of the world" (John 8:12). How, then, could he dwell in her if darkness encompassed her soul? She'd always associated darkness with sin, so perhaps her wrongdoings were to blame and the depression was her fault.

Darkness nearly suffocated Sarah, until she began exploring the Bible for verses that addressed God, light, and darkness. Micah 7:8 marked a turning point for her. The prophet's words helped her realize that God, who is light, never abandons us in the dark. He sits with us and remains our faithful companion in that place.

Biblical truth and medical intervention assured Sarah that her depression was not self-induced. For her, the darkness became the place where God's nearness felt dearer than earthly friendships, and evidences of his goodness shone more brightly. The night became the way for her to find him.

Ponder

How have you experienced God's presence in the nighttime of your soul?

Pray

God, thank you for sitting with me in the dark. I will not fear when you are near.

> "The Spirit of God 'hovered' over the darkness [Genesis 1:1–2]. This Hebrew word is translated as 'moved' and it means to 'shake, flutter, or to relax.' God lived, dwelled, relaxed in the darkness ... God isn't afraid of the dark. God isn't afraid of our darkness. From the beginning God created something 'good' for us—and that includes the darkness. His goodness can be seen even in the hard moments because God is Creator and nothing He creates is bad."
>
> SARAH FRAZER, "How to See God's Light in Times of Darkness"

Superpower

*The Spirit of God, who raised Jesus from the dead,
lives in you. And just as God raised Christ Jesus
from the dead, he will give life to your mortal bodies
by this same Spirit living within you.*

ROMANS 8:11 NLT

Pause

Meet the Incredibles, a cartoon family with superpowers. One stretches like a human elastic band. Another possesses extraordinary strength. Others create force fields, make themselves invisible, or pass through solid objects. They combine their abilities to help people in trouble.

Someone with a good imagination wrote the movie script, and it entertains those who watch it. But here's the thing: when I'm in trouble, I don't want make-believe superheroes to entertain me. I need someone real to rescue me.

The Holy Spirit is that someone. His divine power far exceeds our wildest imagination, and that power lives in us. No problem is too great, no mountain too high. There's nothing he cannot do and no battle he will not fight on our behalf. When we're in trouble, the Holy Spirit and his superpower are only a whisper away.

Ponder

The Holy Spirit's resurrection power lives in you. What difference does this make in your life?

Pray

God, teach me to live day by day from the truth of the Holy Spirit's superpower in me.

"God knows what each one of us is dealing with. He knows our pressures. He knows our conflicts. And He has made a provision for each and every one of them. That provision is Himself in the person of the Holy Spirit, indwelling us and empowering us to respond rightly."

KAY ARTHUR,
As Silver Refined: Learning to Embrace Life's Disappointments

This Storm Will Pass

*[Those caught in storms] mounted up to
the heavens and went down to the depths;
in their peril their courage melted away.
Then they cried out to the LORD in their trouble,
and he brought them out of their distress.*

PSALM 107:26, 28

Pause

Blue skies and gentle breezes beckoned as Sailor-Man and I left the dock, but the marine forecast warned of a storm brewing. Before long, the wind gained strength and black clouds rolled in. Then the monsoon-like downpour began.

Sailor-Man donned rain gear and held his position at the helm. I didn't own rain gear, so I ducked inside. The vessel rocked from side to side. Nausea hit me, and I hung on for dear life. "God, please get us through this," I cried.

Five torturous hours later, the wind subsided, the waves turned to glass, and the sun reappeared. We heaved sighs of gratitude and sipped soda to celebrate.

Storms happen. Sometimes we know they're coming— but not always. Some folks are better prepared and hold steady while others, like me, hang on and cry for mercy. Storms are scary, but the good news is that they don't last forever. The wind will cease, the waves will settle, and the sun will shine again.

Ponder

For what might you be grateful when your storm subsides?

Pray

God, I'm hanging on to you for dear life. Please get me through this.

"Surprises and pitfalls wait for us along the road of life. We're going to sweat and sway, we're going to wonder why things are the way they are. But every road has an end; every mountain has its peak. If we can just hold on and keep climbing, knowing that God is aware of how we're straining, he will bring us up and over the mountains."

THELMA WELLS,
The Best Devotions of Thelma Wells

Nothing Stops God

*Then Job replied to the L*ORD:
"I know that you can do all things;
no purpose of yours can be thwarted."

JOB 42:1–2

𝒫*ause*

A friend interviewed for a job she felt was custom-made for her skills and interests. "I aced it," she said. "I'm so thankful; I really need the income." Her confidence was shattered when the company hired someone else. She wrestled with disappointment and feelings of rejection for a couple of weeks; but then she said, "I don't understand why I didn't get the job, but God must have something better in mind." I wholeheartedly agreed.

God drew up plans for our lives before we were born, and he promises to establish them (Psalm 139:16; Proverbs 16:9). He does so in wisdom and goodness, always with our best interests and his kingdom purposes in mind.

This sweet assurance doesn't promise an easy ride. Disappointments happen. We grieve loss and lost opportunities. But we can be sure of this: God has a plan and nothing stops him from fulfilling it. He never fails or skips a beat. If our perceived best doesn't come to pass, we can be certain something better lies ahead.

Ponder

On a scale of 1 to 10, score your confidence in the truth that nothing thwarts God's purposes for you.

Pray

God, I believe you are sovereign. Help my unbelief.

> "God in His love always wills what is best for us. In His wisdom He always knows what is best, and in His sovereignty He has the power to bring it about."
>
> UNKNOWN SOURCE,
> quoted by Jerry Bridges, *Trusting God*

Set Your Face

Then Jehoshaphat was afraid and set his face to seek the LORD, and proclaimed a fast throughout all Judah.

2 CHRONICLES 20:3 ESV

Pause

King Jehoshaphat was afraid, and for good reason. Several enemy nations had joined forces to fight him and were already headed his way. The situation's seriousness might have caused him to panic and run for cover, but it did not.

Desperate times call for desperate measures. With fervent determination, the king called on God for help; then he declared a nationwide fast and gathered everyone at the Temple to pray. There was no time to delay. Do or die.

Fear is a natural response when we find ourselves in dire straits, and it's okay to admit we're scared. But then let's take decisive action. Let's vigorously seek the Lord through prayer and fasting, and let's call on others to join us.

God is our only hope, and we need him to fight on our behalf. Jehoshaphat's wholehearted dedication to seeking God's help resulted in victory. Setting our face to seek him with fervor is vital to our victory, too. Let's keep our eyes on him and not let discouragement distract us.

Ponder

To what or whom do you turn when you feel afraid? How does that work for you?

Pray

God, help me keep my focus on you alone when I am afraid.

"If I were your enemy, I'd magnify your fears, making them appear insurmountable, intimidating you with enough worries until avoiding them becomes your driving motivation. I would use anxiety to cripple you, to paralyze you, leaving you indecisive, clinging to safety and sameness, always on the defensive because of what might happen. When you hear the word faith, all I'd want you to hear is 'unnecessary risk.'"

PRISCILLA SHIRER,
*Fervent: A Woman's Battle Plan
to Serious Specific, and Strategic Prayer*

Hidden

But if I go to the east, he is not there; if I go to the west,
I do not find him. When he is at work in the north,
I do not see him; when he turns to the south,
I catch no glimpse of him.

JOB 23:8-9

Pause

Great blue herons are common to our marina because we live across the river from a bird sanctuary. One morning, I saw three of these giant birds tiptoeing in the mud. Suddenly one took flight and landed in a tree overhead. I strained for a closeup view, but foliage hid it from sight.

In that instant, a thought came to mind: *The heron is there, even though I can't see it. In the same way, God is real and present, even though I can't see him.*

The analogy echoed Job's response in crisis. He admitted to not being able to see God in his circumstances and then he said, "But he knows the way that I take; when he has tested me, I will come forth as gold" (Job 23:10).

Pain can mask God's presence, but it can't change the truth: he is near, even when we can't see him in our situation.

Ponder

How have circumstances influenced your sense of God's presence?

Pray

God, I trust you're present, even when I can't see you.

> "Trust Him when you cannot trace Him.
> Do not try to penetrate the cloud which He
> 'brings over the earth,' and to look through it.
> Keep your eye steadily fixed on the Bow.
> The mystery is God's, the promise is yours."

JOHN R. MACDUFF,
The Bow in the Cloud: and The First Bereavement

Encouraging Others

"Now I urge you to take some food. You need it to survive. Not one of you will lose a single hair from his head." They were all encouraged and ate some food themselves.

ACTS 27:34, 36

Pause

Paul and 275 other men were in the same boat, and that boat was about to wreck. Two weeks of hurricane-force winds had tossed them about the vessel like human toothpicks. They'd gulped bucketfuls of saltwater and felt its sting on open sores. They'd lost their appetites, their lifeboat, and their hope. Things had never looked so bleak.

Despite his weakened state, Paul focused on his companions' immediate needs. He took bread (guaranteed un-fresh), gave thanks to God, and ate it. Then he shared a promise from God's heart to theirs. His words and actions encouraged the others, and they ate, too.

We don't have to look far to find people in pain. We tend to avoid or overlook them when dealing with our own pain, but let's resolve to be encouragers at all times. A simple kind deed or word (such as, "How can I pray for you?") can work wonders.

Ponder

What's one thing you can do to encourage someone today?

Pray

God, make me aware of and willing to address others' needs, even though I have needs, too.

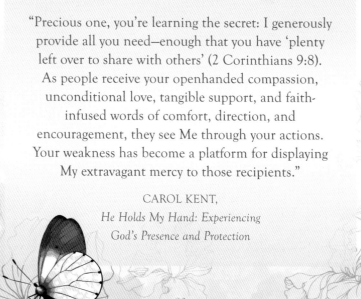

"Precious one, you're learning the secret: I generously provide all you need—enough that you have 'plenty left over to share with others' (2 Corinthians 9:8). As people receive your openhanded compassion, unconditional love, tangible support, and faith-infused words of comfort, direction, and encouragement, they see Me through your actions. Your weakness has become a platform for displaying My extravagant mercy to those recipients."

CAROL KENT,
*He Holds My Hand: Experiencing
God's Presence and Protection*

Belonging to God

Last night an angel of the God to whom I belong
and whom I serve stood beside me and said,
"Do not be afraid, Paul."

ACTS 27:23-24

Pause

Two words describe Paul's voyage during the relentless storm: sheer terror. But one dark and stormy night, God sent hope via an angel. "Don't be afraid," he said. Easier said than done, but Paul found it doable because he knew he belonged to God.

This God was not to be confused with the Egyptian sailors' false gods. This was the all-powerful God who ruled the wind and waves and raised Jesus from the dead. This was the God who'd pursued Paul and adopted him into his family as a son and heir (Romans 8:14–17). He'd become Paul's prayer warrior, strengthened him to rise above persecution and suffering of every sort, and lavished him with unconditional and unending love (Romans 8:28, 31–39). Knowing to whom he belonged filled Paul with confidence that he was in good hands.

When fear comes calling, remind yourself to whom you belong. Remember that God takes responsibility for your well-being. You're in his hands, and fear has no authority to snatch you from them.

Ponder

What specific aspect of God's character brings you courage?

Pray

God, thank you for the sense of security that comes in knowing I belong to you.

"The reason God tries us and tests us is to prove us. He's proving nothing to Himself. He knows us from top to bottom. Instead, He's proving something to *us.* God considers us as valuable as silver, and He puts us into situations that test and strengthen us."

WARREN W. WIERSBE,
Prayer, Praise & Promises:
A Daily Walk through the Psalms

Storms Happen

Keep up your courage, men, for I have faith in God that it will happen just as he told me. Nevertheless, we must run aground on some island.

ACTS 27:25–26

Pause

An angel told Paul that everyone on board his ship would survive the storm, but he also said they would face shipwreck before their saga ended. If I were wearing Paul's sandals, I might be tempted to wonder why this was happening to me. *Did I do something wrong? Is God angry with me? Are evil spiritual forces messing with my life?*

Our nature hunts for answers when bad things happen. There must be a reason, right? Truth is, storms come because we live in a world cursed by sin. Suffering is a direct and universal result of Adam and Eve's choice to disobey God. Therefore, it's not a matter of *if* hardship strikes. It's a matter of *when* (1 Peter 4:12).

Don't spend precious energy trying to figure out why this is happening to you. Instead, thank God that he is sovereign over your circumstances. He knew this was coming, he's aware of your needs, and he's with you right now. He's got this.

Ponder

"God's got this." List the specifics to which this applies in your situation.

Pray

God, I choose to trust you, even though I don't understand why you've allowed this to happen.

"The basic premise of religion—that if you live a good life, things will go well for you—is wrong. Jesus was the most morally upright person who ever lived, yet he had a life filled with the experience of poverty, rejection, injustice, and even torture."

TIMOTHY KELLER,
The Reason for God: Belief in an Age of Skepticism

Jesus' Scars

When the disciples were together, with the doors locked for fear of the Jewish leaders, Jesus came and stood among them and said, "Peace be with you!" After he said this, he showed them his hands and side. The disciples were overjoyed when they saw the Lord.

JOHN 20:19–20

Pause

The disciples huddled in fear behind a locked door. The barrier offered refuge from the religious leaders, but it couldn't provide a sanctuary from the storm in their souls. *What will we do without our beloved teacher? Will we suffer the same fate as his?*

Fear turned to disbelief when Jesus suddenly appeared in their midst and said, "Peace be with you." His greeting cloaked the disciples in calm. But then the Prince of Peace did more than speak reassurance. He showed the men his nail-pierced hands and wounded side.

Jesus' scars reveal the depth of his love for his disciples, for me, and for you. Understanding that love transforms us from people who huddle in fear during the storm to those who possess peace. The nail prints assure us that we are in good hands, and we can trust Jesus no matter what our future holds.

Ponder

What comes to mind when you think about Jesus' scars?

Pray

God, remove any doubt of your love for me and help me live in peace.

"If you want to determine whether God loves you,
don't look at your current situation;
look to the cross."

HENRY BLACKABY AND RICHARD BLACKABY,
Hearing God's Voice

A Strong Foundation

*The rain came down, the streams rose, and the winds
blew and beat against that house; yet it did not fall,
because it had its foundation on the rock.*

MATTHEW 7:25

Pause

Sailor-Man and I often dreamed of owning waterfront property, so we jumped at the opportunity when a lot with a house was listed for sale nearby. Its affordability waved like a cautionary flag, but we ignored it. We wanted to seal the deal before anyone else could beat us to it.

We envisioned remodeling the dilapidated two-story house, but it lacked a foundation. Skilled contractors politely refused to touch this project. In the end, the local fire department burned it, and we built a new house. Construction permits required a foundation able to withstand a minor earthquake.

We learned a costly lesson about the importance of having a proper foundation. The lesson applies to spiritual matters, too. Surviving life's storms requires a strong foundation—faith in the truth about who God is.

God is wise, sovereign, and good. He is faithful to fulfill his promises, and he is able to bring beauty from our brokenness. Living from these truths provides the foundation we need to stand firm.

Ponder

Which of the truths about God's character listed above means the most to you?

Pray

God, protect me from building a faulty foundation and thus learning a costly lesson.

"Faith is deliberate confidence in the character of God whose ways you cannot understand at the time."

OSWALD CHAMBERS,
The Quotable Oswald Chambers

Full Circle

*We know that in all things God works for the
good of those who love him, who have been called
according to his purpose.*

ROMANS 8:28

Pause

Thirteen years of spiritual abuse and manipulation in a
business partnership left wreckage in Athena's life. She lost
her marriage and family, her twenty-year-old publishing
company, and her credit rating. She lost her reputation
and a sound understanding of Scripture. And she nearly
lost her faith.

God began to restore Athena after she broke free from
that toxic relationship. More than anything, she wanted
to marry again, but God said wait. She felt impatient
with his process at times, but he gently loved her back
to emotional, mental, and spiritual health. He addressed
wounds from childhood abuse, a teenage abortion, and
domestic violence. He used counseling and visuals such
as park benches ("Sit down, be still, and think about my

faithfulness") and speed bumps ("Slow down and let me do things my way") to speak truth to her heart.

Athena learned to practice patience, and God eventually granted her desire for a husband. He also gave her a ministry that brings hope to wounded women. He brought her full circle and redeemed her pain for his purposes.

Ponder

What part of your life would you like to see God redeem for his purposes?

Pray

God, redeem my pain and grant me patience in the process.

"God was obviously up to something in my life. I knew He wanted me to slow down. He was at work in the waiting, even when I didn't sense it or enjoy it. He wanted me to pause ... to wait ... to surrender ... to learn to trust Him and His ways ... to keep my eyes focused on Him rather than on what I longed for."

ATHENA DEAN HOLTZ, WITH INGER LOGELIN,
Full Circle: Coming Home to the Faithfulness of God

Day by Day

*He has given me a new song to sing, a hymn of praise to
our God. Many will see what he has done and be amazed.
They will put their trust in the LORD.*

PSALM 40:3

𝒫*ause*

Karolina Sandell-Berg and her father, a pastor, were
crossing a lake in Sweden when the boat suddenly lurched.
Karolina's father fell overboard and drowned before her
eyes. From the depths of her broken heart, she later wrote
numerous hymns of faith. One of the most well-known is
"Day by Day." The first verse goes:

Day by day and with each passing moment,
    Strength I find to meet my trials here;
Trusting in my Father's wise bestowment,
    I've no cause for worry or for fear.
He whose heart is kind beyond all measure,
    Gives unto each day what He deems best—
Lovingly, its part of pain and pleasure,
    Mingling toil with peace and rest.

Karolina's heartache birthed a hymn that has blessed millions because she believed God is good at all times. Can we say that we share her belief? What blessing might God want to birth in us when we hold fast to faith in his goodness?

Ponder

How do the lyrics of "Day by Day" strengthen you today?

Pray

God, you are good to me. Reveal your goodness to others through me.

> "Because God loves us, he gives us lyrics to sing when our hearts can't form words."
>
> JONATHAN PETERSEN

Meditate on Truth

They delight in the law of the LORD, meditating on it day and night. They are like trees planted along the riverbank, bearing fruit each season. Their leaves never wither, and they prosper in all they do.

PSALM 1:2–3 NLT

Pause

Neuroscience and the Bible agree that our thoughts' habitual focus determines what we become. I've found this to be true when dealing with difficult circumstances. If I fall asleep ruminating about my worries, I wake in the morning with a feeling of heaviness and dread. In contrast, I wake up feeling at peace if I fall asleep meditating on Bible verses and various aspects of God's character the night before.

Dwelling on God's character and promises literally renews our brain and leads to personal transformation (Rom. 12:2). Hopeful anticipation of a good outcome replaces fear and dread. An awareness of others' needs replaces a tendency toward self-focus. Even our speech changes as gratitude and encouragement replace complaints.

Delighting in God's truth day and night deepens our faith and develops our faith story. It turns a difficult season of our life into one that blossoms with new personal growth and can result in new friendships and opportunities. It all begins with the thoughts we habitually think.

Ponder

What thoughts would you like to change?

Pray

God, help me learn to dwell on your truth rather than my difficulties.

"What you are thinking every moment of every day becomes a physical reality in your brain and body, which affects your optimal mental and physical health. These thoughts collectively form your attitude, which is your state of mind, and it's your attitude and not your DNA that determines much of the quality of your life."

CAROLINE LEAF, *Switch On Your Brain: The Key to Peak Happiness, Thinking, and Health*

God Loves, Sees, Cares

I will be glad and rejoice in your unfailing love,
for you have seen my troubles, and you care
about the anguish of my soul.

PSALM 31:7 NLT

Pause

Sara and her twenty-something granddaughter, Anna, had been collaborating long-distance on a book proposal when communication suddenly went dark. Unanswered emails and calls left Sara feeling anxious, hurt, and confused. *How can someone so dear cut off contact without an explanation?* she wondered. *Have I offended her? Is she in trouble?*

In desperation, Sara began praying Scripture promises on Anna's behalf. She found consolation in remembering that God loved her granddaughter more than she ever could. She clung to three truths found in Psalm 31:7—God loved her, he saw her in her hard place, and he cared about her hurt. Choosing to believe these spiritual realities carried her through fifty-three agonizing days before Anna phoned and revealed her private struggle with depression.

Life's uncertainties often leave us with more questions than answers, but of this we can be sure: God loves us, sees us in our hard place, and cares about our hurt. Living as though we believe these things are true always fills us with hope.

Ponder

Which of the three truths in Psalm 31:7 resonates most with you? Why?

Pray

God, I have questions about my circumstances, but I don't question your love.

"At times it may feel as if we are helpless to what happens to us, and that things happen without rhyme or reason. Rest assured that no matter how choppy the sea gets or how the wind blows, Jesus is on the boat."

TIFFANY JACKSON, *12 Keys to Success for Misfits, Weirdos and Introverts*

Moral Support

The first time I was brought before the judge,
no one came with me. Everyone abandoned me.
May it not be counted against them.

2 TIMOTHY 4:16 NLT

Pause

The apostle Paul felt abandoned when no one came to lend moral support as he stood trial before Nero. Maybe you, too, have felt forgotten in your hour of need.

We all appreciate receiving support in difficult times, but friends might disappoint us. Harboring negative emotions toward them for not fulfilling our expectations can lead to anger, self-pity, and bitterness.

Paul refused to go that direction. Instead, he asked God to not hold anything against his friends. He also acknowledged God's faithfulness: "But the Lord stood with me and gave me strength so that I might preach the Good News in its entirety for all the Gentiles to hear. And he rescued me from certain death" (2 Timothy 4:17 NLT).

We can't control the response of others to us in our hour of need, but we can control our response to feeling forgotten. Following Paul's example of praying for our friends is a good start. We can also move past disappointment by remembering God's faithfulness to us. His support gives us the strength we need to survive our trials.

$\mathcal{P}$onder

Identify one way in which God has stood by you in this trial.

$\mathcal{P}$ray

God, thank you for never leaving my side during my hour of need.

"Keep your eyes on Christ,
not the circumstances you find yourself in
or the feelings you are experiencing."

BRUCE WILKINSON,
*You Were Born for This: 7 Keys to a
Life of Predictable Miracles*

My Hiding Place

You are my hiding place; you will protect me from trouble
and surround me with songs of deliverance.

PSALM 32:7

Pause

Sailor-Man and I toured Corrie ten Boom's childhood home in the Netherlands. I will never forget crawling on hands and knees through Corrie's bedroom closet to enter the secret room where Jews hid from Nazi soldiers during WWII. The hiding place held six standing adults—not a comfortable space, but well-concealed and safe.

The psalmist described God as his hiding place. When he felt assailed by enemies like fear and shame, he ran to God as to a secret room and found refuge. The presence and peace of God filled him with courage, strength, and hope.

We, too, can run to God as our hiding place in times of uncertainty and fear. How do we do this? By reading his promises, listening to praise and worship music, and giving him our concerns. We do it by turning to him for help first, not as a last resort, and by speaking aloud truth like Psalm 32:7.

God alone is our hiding place. Run to him. Take refuge in his presence. Find courage in his promises. You will find security there, and there he will surround you with songs of deliverance.

$\mathcal{P}$onder

Identify the enemy from which you need to hide.

$\mathcal{P}$ray

God, I'm running to you. Be my safe place.

"Where does your security lie? That's my question for you today. Is God your refuge, your hiding place, your stronghold, your shepherd, your counselor, your friend, your redeemer, your savior, your guide? If He is, you don't need to search any further for security."

ELISABETH ELLIOT,
The Search for Security: Security in God

When Paths Intersect

Pause

"What brought you here?" I asked the woman whose child shared an ICU room with mine. The stranger whose path had intersected mine a couple hours earlier began telling me her story.

The bond that began with a simple question grew over several days as we sat by our children's bedsides. When the nurses urged us to take a break, I invited my new friend to join me for lunch. Conversation deepened over soup and salad. After she shared some matters of the heart, I asked permission to pray for her. Her eyes widened. "You would do that?" she asked. "Of course," I replied. I kept it short and simple, but it was enough to encourage her during that stressful time.

It's no accident when paths intersect. Perhaps God has placed you where you are so that you can encourage someone hungry for hope. Keep your eyes open for the person whose path crosses yours, and trust the Holy Spirit to show you how to respond. It doesn't have to be complicated. Sometimes a listening ear or simple prayer is enough.

Ponder

Whose path has intersected yours in recent days?

Pray

God, bring someone who needs hope across my path today.

> "You have no idea how many people there are in the world whose day could be made and their life changed for the better if someone would just look them in the eye, smile, and say, 'Hello.'"

STORMIE OMARTIAN,
30 Days to Becoming a Woman of Prayer

When in Doubt

[Thomas] said to them, "Unless I see the nail marks
in his hands and put my finger where the nails were,
and put my hand into his side, I will not believe."
Then [Jesus] said to Thomas, "Put your finger here;
see my hands. Reach out your hand and put it
into my side. Stop doubting and believe."

JOHN 20:25, 27

Pause

Human nature makes it hard for us to trust what we don't understand. Difficulties come our way and we begin to doubt God's wisdom, sovereignty, and goodness. We question his intent toward us. We doubt his presence with us. We might keep those doubts to ourselves, but he knows everything about them.

Jesus knew Thomas's doubts, even though he wasn't physically present when the disciple expressed them. Jesus also knew precisely how to address those doubts, and he met Thomas at his point of need.

Perhaps you have a few doubts of your own at this time. Be aware that God knows the thoughts we entertain. Be aware, too, that our thoughts matter to him. He's more than willing to answer our questions and settle our doubts, so we can declare with certainty as Thomas did, "My Lord and my God!" (John 20:28).

Ponder

What doubts do you have at this time?

Pray

God, I know you love me. Please settle all doubts about your intent toward me.

"The secret to joy is to keep seeking God where we doubt He is."

ANN VOSKAMP,
One Thousand Gifts: A Dare to Live Fully Right Where You Are

Scary Situations

You, God, are my God, earnestly I seek you;
I thirst for you, my whole being longs for you,
in a dry and parched land where there is no water.

PSALM 63:1

Pause

My prayer life deepened the first time I rode a bus leaving Nepal's Kathmandu Valley. It carried more passengers than seats inside, and the overflow sat on the roof. Each time the vehicle rounded a curve, I envisioned this top-heavy vehicle toppling down the mountainside. To say I was scared is a gross understatement. To say I sought God earnestly is no exaggeration.

Scary situations aren't something we pursue, but sometimes we can't avoid them. They stretch our faith and test our Sunday school theology. They become the proving ground for what we profess to believe. They can potentially produce new growth and prune the old.

That bus ride made me desperate for God. I wanted him near more than anything in the world. Other faith-testing situations have come and gone since then, and they, too, have cast me on the Lord. My human nature would rather avoid such circumstances, but I'm learning that any experience that creates a desperation for God is an opportunity to know him more intimately.

Ponder

What situation has made you desperate for God?

Pray

God, I pray not for an easy life but for a deep life.

"Though my natural instinct is to wish for a life free from pain, trouble, and adversity, I am learning to welcome anything that makes me conscious of my need for Him. If prayer is birthed out of desperation, then anything that makes me desperate for God is a blessing."

NANCY DEMOSS WOLGEMUTH,
The Quiet Place: Daily Devotional Readings

Our Source of Hope

*Let all that I am wait quietly before God, for my
hope is in him. He alone is my rock and my salvation,
my fortress where I will not be shaken.*

PSALM 62:5-6 NLT

Pause

I read a story about a group of friends who discussed playing the lottery. Some called it gambling. Others called it a game. The discussion grew more animated until one fellow said quietly, "It's a hope-giver. That's why people play the lottery. Everyone wants hope, right?"

It's true: everyone wants hope, and people look for it in different places. Some search for it in self-help books and courses. Others think they'll find it in a relationship. Some people believe money or material possessions will bring it. Some would feel hopeful if their health or the weather improved, or if life would return to the normal we all once knew. The list goes on.

The truth is, only God brings the hope for which our hearts yearn. He remains in control when our circumstances appear to spin out of control. He remains steadfast and immovable when our world shakes and falls apart. He remains faithful when people disappoint or betray us.

Hang in there. God will come through in his time and in his way.

Ponder

In whom or what, other than God, have you sought hope?

Pray

God, my hope is in you alone.

"Hope doesn't announce that life is safe, therefore, we will be; instead, it whispers that Christ is our safety in the midst of harsh reality."

PATSY CLAIRMONT,
Dancing Bones: Living Lively in the Valley

Looking to Jesus

When [Peter] saw the wind, he was afraid and,
beginning to sink, cried out, "Lord, save me!"
Immediately Jesus reached out his hand
and caught him. "You of little faith," he said,
"why did you doubt?"

MATTHEW 14:30–31

Pause

Sailor-Man and I had invited another couple to join us for
a three-day sailing trip. They'd never done anything like
it, so their eyes grew wide a few times. When we motored
through rapids and whirlpools caused by tidal action, I saw
my friend grip her husband's arm. That's when I shared
a hint that I've found helpful: look at the captain, not at
the waves.

Fixing my eyes on whitecaps and whirlpools always makes
me imagine the worst. But fixing my eyes on Sailor-Man has
the opposite effect. His calm demeanor says, *All is well.*
Everything's under control.

The apostle Peter walked on stormy seas when he focused on the Savior. The moment his focus shifted, the waves threatened to swallow him. They'll swallow us, too, if we fixate on them. The key to facing our circumstances with calm is to keep our eyes on Jesus. His calm demeanor says, *Everything's under control—my control. All is well.*

Ponder

Jesus asked Peter why he doubted him. What doubts do you have about Jesus?

Pray

God, fill my vision with only you.

"Are you in a hurry, flurried, distressed? Look up! See the Man in the Glory! Let the face of Jesus shine upon you—the face of the Lord Jesus Christ. Is He worried, troubled, distressed? There is no wrinkle on His brow, no least shade of anxiety. Yet the affairs are His as much as yours."

HOWARD TAYLOR AND MRS. HOWARD TAYLOR,
*Hudson Taylor and the China Inland Mission:
The Growth of a Work of God*

A Path Unseen

Pause

A random collection of cars, pickups, tractor trailers, and RVs jammed the two-lane highway on which Sailor-Man and I were driving. Suddenly the vehicles ahead of us parted like a zipper being undone. Sailor-Man glanced in the rear-view mirror and, seeing flashing red lights, immediately followed suit. Seconds later, an ambulance sped past on a lane that hadn't existed moments earlier.

Congested traffic parting for an emergency vehicle seemed an impressive sight, but that was nothing compared to the Red Sea parting for the Israelites (Exodus 14:21–22). The people had no idea the escape route was there until God made it appear at the exact moment they needed it most.

My friend, perhaps you feel like you're in a jam. Trouble surrounds you on every side and you feel like there's nowhere to turn. Time is running out as the enemy presses in.

Do not be afraid! God knows the way of escape. You can't see the path, but he knows where it is, and he'll show it to you at the exact moment you need to know it.

Ponder

What obstacles do you think God must remove to create your escape route?

Pray

God, in your perfect timing, please make a path where I see none.

"God has promised that whatever you face, you are not alone. He knows your pain. He loves you. And He will bring you through the fire."

SHEILA WALSH,
The Storm Inside: Trade the Chaos of How You Feel for the Truth of Who You Are

Peace in the Valley

*Even though I walk through the valley of the shadow
of death, I fear no evil, for You are with me;
Your rod and Your staff, they comfort me.*

PSALM 23:4 NASB

Pause

Sirens screamed as the ambulance arrived at Heidi and Jack's house. Inside, Heidi was performing CPR on her husband after he'd collapsed on the kitchen floor. The medics were able to restore Jack's pulse before transporting him to the hospital, but he died five days later.

Heidi was all-too-familiar with the dark valley of the shadow of death: she'd lost her first husband to cardiac arrest two decades before this. Now she walked the path again, but this time for her beloved Jack. Her heart shattered and grief defied words, but in the midst of this crisis, she experienced an inexplicable peace.

Human logic could not explain the peace that pervaded Heidi's heart and mind as she bid her husband goodbye.

She knew the future would be hard, but she also knew she would not go there alone. Jesus had promised to never leave or forsake her. He would walk that road with her, comforting and guiding her every step of the way.

Ponder

What, or who, brings you peace in the dark valley?

Pray

God, make me keenly aware of your presence before, beside, and behind me as I walk this path.

"Our awesome God wants to be your helper and to guide you through every storm. It doesn't mean you won't feel excruciating pain, disappointment, rejection, or failure. But it does mean you don't have to walk through the storms alone."

HEIDI MCLAUGHLIN,
Fresh Joy: Finding Joy in the Midst of Loss,
Hardship and Suffering

When Plans Change

In their hearts humans plan their course,
but the LORD establishes their steps.

PROVERBS 16:9

Pause

The day dawned with the promise of a smooth sail home. Sailor-Man estimated a seven-hour trip, if everything went according to plan. His estimate fell only fifty-three hours short.

By day's end, the engine had failed three times. The dinghy we tow in case of an emergency had been punctured. The electronic gizmo that raises the anchor had broken. When we finally limped into the nearest marina at midnight, Canadian border guards searched our boat for drugs and threatened us with six months in prison or a $750,000 fine for crossing into US waters and then re-entering Canada during COVID. By that time, I didn't know whether to laugh or cry. Thankfully, after they heard our story, they reconsidered and let us go.

We make plans, but circumstances beyond our control change them in a heartbeat. Things go from bad to worse. Before long, our lives look so chaotic that we don't know whether to laugh or cry.

It's always good to remember who's in charge. We make our plans, but the Lord reigns. Living from this truth helps us survive the ride, especially when nothing goes as we expect.

Ponder

What's your usual response when plans change and everything seems to go wrong? How does Proverbs 16:9 encourage you?

Pray

God, guard my heart from anxiety when you overrule my plans.

"We can find ourselves in the middle of God's perfect will and in the middle of a perfect storm at the same time!"

DAVID JEREMIAH, *What Are You Afraid Of? Facing Down Your Fears with Faith*

Reframed

*Sorrowful, yet always rejoicing; poor, yet making many rich;
having nothing, and yet possessing everything.*

2 CORINTHIANS 6:10

Pause

The apostle Paul took a beating in ministry both physically and emotionally. When we read his hardships listed in 2 Corinthians 6:4–5, we might be tempted to say, "Whoa! That's brutal. How could anyone endure such things and not quit?"

In today's key verse, Paul described his state of being after suffering those afflictions. Three times he used the word *yet*. If we omit it and everything behind it, we find Paul sorrowful, poor, and having nothing. Grim, right? But the opposite is true.

Paul reframed his difficulties. Hardships could not defeat him because he lived in the power of Christ who said, "I am the resurrection, and the life: he that believeth in me, though he were dead, yet shall he live" (John 11:25 KJV).

Without Christ, we are nothing, we have nothing, we hope for nothing. But Christ's resurrection reframes us. We still face hardships, but we do so with a *yet*. We can be sorrowful *yet* joy filled. Poor *yet* profit others. Destitute *yet* wealthy. Weak *yet* strong. Crushed *yet* not destroyed.

Ponder

Complete this sentence: I am _____ *yet* _____.

Pray

God, help me live in the power of Christ and the hope of *yet*.

"God has given us a purpose for our existence, a reason to go on, even though that existence includes tough times. Living through suffering, we become sanctified—in other words, set apart for the glory of God. We gain perspective. We grow deeper. We grow up!"

CHARLES R. SWINDOLL,
Hope Again: When Life Hurts and Dreams Fade

Persevere

Blessed is the one who perseveres under trial
because, having stood the test, that person will
receive the crown of life that the Lord has
promised to those who love him.

JAMES 1:12

Pause

Attending a summer camp in British Columbia in my early twenties pushed me far beyond my comfort zone. One day, the schedule included hiking up a bluff. The path wound through ferns and old forest growth before beginning a steep ascent along a rock face.

The path narrowed and the pace slowed. I edged my way up the trail with no margin for error. A single glance downward shot fear through my body. *I can't do this*, I thought. More than once I wanted to turn back, but others came behind me. The only way out was up.

Perhaps you sometimes feel like you can't do this anymore. The path is far too hard. May I encourage you to press on?

When I finally reached the summit, the panoramic view of pristine lakes, mountain ridges, and forests made every painstaking step worthwhile. You'll find every step worthwhile, too, when the Lord rewards you with the crown of life.

Ponder

A crown awaits you! How does this promise bring you strength?

Pray

God, please give me strength to do this, and do it well, for the duration.

> "When you face a mountain in your life, you have a choice: be overwhelmed or be energized because you know the Savior will reveal Himself in a profound way to you."
>
> CHARLES F. STANLEY,
> *Every Day in His Presence*

Friends

*Elijah was afraid and fled for his life. He went to
Beersheba, a town in Judah, and he left his servant
there. Then he went on alone into the wilderness,
traveling all day.*

1 KINGS 19:3–4 NLT

Pause

Elijah and his servant fled together from Queen Jezebel's
death threat but eventually parted ways. Perhaps the
servant couldn't match Elijah's pace. Maybe Elijah felt
that separating was safer for the servant's sake. Perhaps
the servant believed they'd reached a refuge, but panic
pushed Elijah on. Regardless of the reason, the prophet
entered the wilderness alone. Here's what happened next:
"he sat down under a solitary broom tree and prayed that
he might die" (1 Kings 19:4 NLT).

Sometimes life is too hard to go it alone. God is with us,
yes, but we need friends, too. We might think handling
our situation alone spares them inconvenience. We might
believe they don't need another thing on their plate. We

might even think no one cares enough to listen or pray or help, so going solo is best. But is it?

Isolating ourselves in the storm makes us vulnerable to the enemy's attacks. Even Jesus took friends with him to the Garden of Gethsemane before his arrest (Matthew 26:36). If *he* needed friends in a crisis, we need them more.

Ponder

List the friends on whom you can rely for support.

Pray

God, guard my heart from believing I can do this on my own.

"The Spirit of God lives inside of me, and because of that, I'm never alone. There are people who love me, who want to be with me. I can reach out to them instead of sitting here, stuck."

JENNIE ALLEN,
Get Out of Your Head: Stopping the Spiral of Toxic Thoughts

A Fresh Revelation

The LORD said, "Go out and stand on the
mountain in the presence of the LORD,
for the LORD is about to pass by."

1 KINGS 19:11

Pause

Elijah had just seen God accomplish a miraculous victory over those who worshiped Baal, but then Queen Jezebel threatened him with death. Her death warrant undid him. His thoughts spiraled downward until he prayed to die. Think about it: he fled for his life and then asked God to let him die. Go figure.

Elijah's negative mindset was still evident more than a month later when he described his situation to God. We might have expected God to say, "Wait a minute. Think again. You've got it all wrong." Instead, he gave Elijah a fresh revelation of his character (1 Kings 19:11–12).

Sometimes we need a fresh revelation of God, too. As happened to Elijah, our perception can become skewed when we suffer and focus on the hardship at hand. In times like this, we don't need God to give us a detailed explanation of what's really happening. His words would likely land on deaf ears. What we really need is a fresh glimpse of his power to strengthen us, his grace to carry us, and his love to hold us.

Ponder

What fresh revelation of God's character do you want most?

Pray

God, adjust my perspective through the truth of who you are.

"When you and I hurt deeply, what we really need is not an explanation from God but a revelation of God. We need to see how great God is; we need to recover our lost perspective on life. Things get out of proportion when we are suffering, and it takes a vision of something bigger than ourselves to get life's dimensions adjusted again."

WARREN W. WIERSBE,
Looking Up When Life Gets You Down

Light in the Darkness

If I say, "Surely the darkness will hide me and the light become night around me," even the darkness will not be dark to you; the night will shine like the day, for darkness is as light to you.

PSALM 139:11–12

Pause

My imagination ran rampant in the dark when I was a child. It convinced me that monsters hid under furniture and around every corner, waiting to grab unsuspecting souls. The basement was especially scary. If I had to fetch something for Mom, I always turned on the light at the top of the stairs first. Darkness and fear vanished the instant light appeared.

Now decades later, darkness still makes me uneasy—but not the physical kind. Perhaps you can relate. Sometimes darkness descends and envelops the soul. It blocks us from seeing the truth about ourselves and our circumstances. Our imagination runs rampant, and we begin to believe it portrays the truth when in reality, it's far from it. The result? We fear the worst.

In times like this, let's remember that God is with us, even in life's dark places (Psalm 139:9–10). Living from the truth of his presence and promises punctuates our night with his light and dispels our fear.

Ponder

What is your imagination telling you about your circumstances?

Pray

God, be the light that dispels the darkness around me.

"It is in the dark that God is passing by. The bridge and our lives shake not because God has abandoned, but the exact opposite: God is passing by. God is in the tremors. Dark is the holiest ground, the glory passing by. In the blackest, God is closest, at work, forging His perfect and right will. Though it is black and we can't see and our world seems to be free-falling and we feel utterly alone, Christ is most present to us."

ANN VOSKAMP, *One Thousand Gifts: A Dare to Live Fully Right Where You Are*

Spiritual Warfare

Our struggle is not against flesh and blood,
but against the rulers, against the authorities,
against the powers of this dark world and against
the spiritual forces of evil in the heavenly realms.

EPHESIANS 6:12

Pause

I pray daily for God to do a deep cleansing and freeing work in a woman who frequently targets me with criticism. Mounting frustration over not seeing change came to a head one day, and I finally asked, "C'mon, Lord, what's the hindrance?"

The Holy Spirit whispered, "This battle isn't against flesh and blood. This is spiritual warfare." His words helped me realize that I'd begun viewing the woman as my enemy. The truth is, she's not my enemy. Satan is. He is, in fact, our common enemy.

Satan is determined to cause family feuds between God's children. When relationship tensions arise, we must be aware of Satan's ploys. If he can deceive us into believing that the other person is our enemy, then we forget who the real foe is. We drop our guard and become vulnerable to attack on another front.

When there's friction in the flock, remember who the real enemy is and fight him instead. Heaven's spiritual forces are on your side.

Ponder

Complete this sentence: My real enemy is Satan, not

_____.

Pray

God, make me battle-wise, always aware that one of my true enemy's tactics is to divide and conquer.

"The devil, darkness, and death may swagger and boast, the pangs of life will sting for a while longer, but don't worry; the forces of evil are breathing their last. So there's no need to worry ... He has risen!"

CHARLES R. SWINDOLL,
"Not to Worry ... He's Risen,"
Insight for Living Ministries

Pain's Purpose

*You intended to harm me, but God intended it
for good to accomplish what is now being done,
the saving of many lives.*

GENESIS 50:20

*P*ause

Joseph experienced more hardship in his young adult years than most people know in a lifetime. First, his jealous brothers sold him into slavery. Then a woman's false accusations destroyed his reputation and sent him to prison. Despite the warden's considering him trustworthy, Joseph endured much suffering there. "They bruised his feet with fetters and placed his neck in an iron collar" (Psalm 105:18 NLT).

God used pain to refine and shape Joseph's character (Psalm 105:19). Adversity matured him to fill a strategic position that years later enabled him to save many lives during a famine. It also worked a mighty miracle in his personal life. The proof lies in his ability to forgive his brothers for their betrayal and to treat them and their families kindly, even after their father died.

Our human nature wants to wish pain away as quickly as possible, but remember that God has a purpose for it. When we're willing to let him bring that purpose to pass, he will give us patience and the power to persevere.

Ponder

What character quality might God want to perfect in you through your pain?

Pray

God, take my pain away but only after you've fulfilled your purpose for it.

"Adversity, however, is not simply a tool. It is God's most effective tool for the advancement of our spiritual lives. The circumstances and events that we see as setbacks are oftentimes the very things that launch us into periods of intense spiritual growth. Once we begin to understand this, and accept it as a spiritual fact of life, adversity becomes easier to bear."

CHARLES STANLEY,
How to Handle Adversity

Jehovah Sabaoth

David said to the Philistine, "You come against me with sword and spear and javelin, but I come against you in the name of the LORD Almighty, the God of the armies of Israel, whom you have defied."

1 SAMUEL 17:45

Pause

The name *LORD Almighty* comes from the Hebrew *Jehovah Sabaoth*. It recognizes God as commander-in-chief over all heavenly and earthly armies. When David faced Goliath, he used that name as a declaration of God's undefeatable power over every enemy, whether physical or spiritual. The giant and his weapons looked impressive by human standards, but David may have seen him more as a neighborhood bully wearing a dress-up costume and playing a soldier game.

Understanding the meaning of this name has transformed the way I view my giants. I used to let them intimidate me as they towered above and cast their shadow over me—

but no more. Now I see them dwarfed in the shadow of Jehovah Sabaoth.

When giants of any description loom over us, we needn't be afraid. Jehovah Sabaoth lives in us, and his power can never be defeated. Victory is ours when we call on his name.

Ponder

How does understanding the meaning of *Jehovah Sabaoth* change the way you see your giant?

Pray

God, I stand in your shadow and in the power of your mighty name.

"If the Lord be with us, we have not cause of fear. His eye is upon us, his arm over us, his ear open to our prayer; his grace sufficient, his promise unchangeable."

JOHN NEWTON,
The Works of the Rev. John Newton

145

A Future Hope

There is surely a future hope for you,
and your hope will not be cut off.

PROVERBS 23:18

Pause

How could gall bladder surgery go so wrong? Lyli thought. Every possible post-op complication the surgeon had mentioned had become a reality. To make matters worse, medicine prescribed to heal had worked the opposite way and sent her spiraling into depression and insomnia.

Lyli suffered physically, mentally, and emotionally for more than a year. At one point, she thought she'd never sleep well again without taking a pill first. Her future looked bleak, and she feared she might lose her marriage, her job as an educator, everything. In desperation, she opened her Bible and read Proverbs 23:18. Reassured that God held her future in his loving hands, she refused to give up. Eventually, a Christian psychiatrist prescribed a different medication to promote healing, and Lyli's story made a turn for the better.

Circumstances might leave us asking, "How could things go so wrong?" Our lives spiral in a direction we'd never anticipated, and we fear what the future holds. In times like these, God's promises strengthen our grip and help us persevere. We hold on to hope, knowing he holds our future in his nail-scarred hands.

Ponder

Have you placed your future in God's nail-scarred hands? If not, do it now.

Pray

God, I trust you with the future, knowing you're already there.

"Though we may not be able to see his purpose
or his plan, the Lord of heaven
is on his throne and in firm control
of the universe and our lives."

MAX LUCADO,
*America Looks Up: Reaching toward Heaven
for Hope and Healing*

Strength for the Weary

Come to me, all you who are weary and burdened,
and I will give you rest. Take my yoke upon you and
learn from me, for I am gentle and humble in heart,
and you will find rest for your souls.

MATTHEW 11:28–29

Pause

For three months during the pandemic, Sailor-Man and I moved in with our youngest daughter to help her through a difficult pregnancy. My empty-nester writing life shifted to caring for her toddler, preparing meals, and running errands. I hadn't seen this change of pace coming when I'd accepted several writing assignments and committed to teaching a weekly Zoom Bible study.

I woke early every morning and faced a decision: sleep longer or spend time with God. The former tempted me, but the latter drew me. I read God's Word and invited his presence and power into my day. He blessed me with strength according to the need.

Jesus offers rest for the weary, but there's one caveat: we must come to him to receive it. Doing so can be difficult when chaos hits, but carving out a few moments to be quiet in his presence—if only to exhale our concerns and inhale his peace—is time well spent.

Ponder

What makes you bone-weary?

Pray

God, strength for today's needs, please. I trust your supply one day at a time.

"No soul can be really at rest until it has given up all dependence on everything else and has been forced to depend on the Lord alone. As long as our expectation is from other things, nothing but disappointment awaits us."

HANNAH WHITALL SMITH,
The God of All Comfort

Close to His Heart

[God] will feed his flock like a shepherd.
He will carry the lambs in his arms,
holding them close to his heart. He will gently lead
the mother sheep with their young.

ISAIAH 40:11 NLT

Pause

My son-in-law, David, carried an infant car seat holding his newborn son into the house and set it near me. Then he asked, "Do you want to hold him?" Does a fish swim?

David scooped up one-day-old Joshua and passed him to me. I welcomed my newest grandchild into my arms and retreated to a rocking chair. There I sat and cradled him close to my heart. Swaddled in a new blanket and sound asleep, he personified peace.

When I'm stressed or afraid, I use my sanctified imagination and envision myself cradled in Jesus' arms, close to his heart. I feel enveloped by his love. Protected. Shielded. I feel safe, and peace replaces anxiety.

Isn't it reassuring to know that Jesus really does hold us? This is truth, not just a feel-good exercise of the imagination. We're in his arms, close to his heart, and there's no better place to be.

Ponder

Do as I do, and envision yourself cradled in Jesus' arms, close to his heart. Bask in the beauty of this image.

Pray

God, hold me close and help me know the peace of your nearness.

"Wherever you are spiritually, whatever you have been through emotionally, you are already wrapped in the Lord's embrace. Held by nail-scarred hands. Enfolded in the arms of One who believes in you, supports you, treasures you, and loves you."

LIZ CURTIS HIGGS,
Embrace Grace: Welcome to the Forgiven Life

Honesty and Health

David pleaded with God for the child.
He fasted and spent the nights lying in
sackcloth on the ground.

2 SAMUEL 12:16

Pause

A friend who has faced numerous tragedies told me that trying to appear emotionally strong in their wake was a mistake. She admitted to wearing a plastic smile and telling people that she was fine when, in reality, the opposite was true. That repeated response to hardship eventually took its toll, and depression enveloped her.

Acknowledging our difficulties and giving ourselves the grace and space to process them is vital to our well-being. King David realized and modeled this when his infant son became deathly ill. Rather than trying to appear stoic and carry on with royal responsibilities, he withdrew to spend time alone with God. He prayed and fasted for the child's life, and he grieved the sin of adultery in which this baby had been conceived.

David's honesty before God and others helped him deal with his son's death in a healthy way. Let's be honest, too. Let's acknowledge when we're having a hard time and allow ourselves the freedom to process what's happening. We aren't doing ourselves or anyone else a favor when we pretend that everything's okay when it's not.

Ponder

How do you respond when others ask how you're doing?

Pray

God, help me respond to my situation in a way that promotes health and healing.

> "It is not right, therefore, for us to simply say to a person in grief and sorrow that they need to pull themselves together. We should be more gentle and patient with them. And that means we should also be gentle and patient with ourselves. We should not assume that if we are trusting in God we won't weep, or feel anger, or feel hopeless."
>
> TIMOTHY KELLER, *Walking with God through Pain and Suffering*

Flourish

*As a mother comforts her child, so will [the LORD]
comfort you.... When you see this, your heart will rejoice
and you will flourish like grass.*

ISAIAH 66:13–14

Pause

Margaret stood in an internet café in Nairobi, her hand trembling as she held the phone. "This is the Brantford General Hospital," said the caller. "Your husband passed away one hour ago." The news shocked her and her two adult children. They'd traveled to Kenya on a mission trip, knowing their husband and father was ill but assured that he'd be fine in their absence.

The trio limped to their hotel where Margaret opened her Bible. Isaiah 66:13–14 instantly came to mind. She understood the promise of comfort, but the phrase "you will flourish" puzzled her. How was that even possible midst searing pain and loss?

The answer came that night in Chris Tomlin's song "How Great Is Our God." The lyrics ran through Margaret's mind and focused her thoughts on God's great power and faithfulness. They bathed her heart with hope, reassuring her that God had led her to this season of sorrow, and he would lead her out. She knew sorrow would pass, and she would someday flourish again.

Ponder

What song brings you hope for the future?

Pray

God, I have trouble believing that I will one day flourish again, but I believe you will do it.

"What we learn in one life season prepares us for the next. Don't confuse the pain of the present with your potential. Trust the power of God to bring you through a highly emotional and stressful season into a new one where you will flourish."

MARGARET GIBB

Our Rescuer

Surely God is my salvation; I will trust and
not be afraid. The LORD, the LORD himself,
is my strength and my defense;
he has become my salvation.

ISAIAH 12:2

Pause

Every time Sailor-Man and I cruise British Columbia's coastline, I hear boaters in distress, speaking on the VHF radio. Typically, they're experiencing either engine failure, a fire on board, or a man overboard. They need immediate assistance, and they can only hope for a rapid response from a nearby boater or the Coast Guard.

When tough circumstances have caused me distress, I've sought help from various sources. I've turned to a bag of chips or a dish of ice cream for comfort. I've gone shopping and called it retail therapy. I've texted my SOS to a friend or posted my cry for help on social media.

Don't do what I've done. Trust me. Those things have never rescued me.

I've learned that God alone is our salvation when we're in trouble. He's never too busy or too far away to come to our rescue. The Lord, the Lord himself is our savior. When we call for help, he's always near and ready to save us in our distress.

Ponder

To what or to whom do you send an SOS when you're in distress?

Pray

God, hear my cries for help and rescue me.

"Whether Jesus calms the storm or
calms us in the storm, His love is the same,
and His grace is enough."

SHEILA WALSH,
*Extraordinary Faith: God's Perfect Gift
for Every Woman's Heart*

God's Strength

You are my strength, I sing praise to you;
you, God, are my fortress,
my God on whom I can rely.

PSALM 59:17

Pause

Caring for her elderly mother while working full time as the women's ministry director at a large church left my friend Crickett utterly depleted. On one occasion, she returned home in the wee hours of the morning, exhausted after yet another trip to the hospital emergency room for her mom's sake. *I can't do this much longer*, she thought.

Aware of her inadequacy and of her desperate need for God, Crickett dug into Scripture and discovered these words: "But I will sing of your strength, in the morning I will sing of your love; for you are my fortress, my refuge in times of trouble" (Psalm 59:16). The psalm helped Crickett shift her focus from her weakness to God's strength and sufficiency. She began praising him for who he is. Doing so rejuvenated her body and restored her hope.

Seasons in life come and go, and some leave us depleted. Those difficult times reveal our weakness, but they're often the conduit through which God reveals his strength.

Ponder

The psalmist sung about God's strength and love. What's the theme of your song?

Pray

God, I see my weakness. Open my eyes to behold your strength.

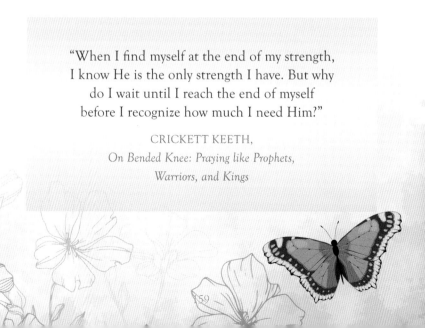

"When I find myself at the end of my strength, I know He is the only strength I have. But why do I wait until I reach the end of myself before I recognize how much I need Him?"

CRICKETT KEETH,
On Bended Knee: Praying like Prophets, Warriors, and Kings

God of Heaven

When I heard this, I sat down and wept.
In fact, for days I mourned, fasted,
and prayed to the God of heaven.

NEHEMIAH 1:4

Pause

Visitors bearing bad news from Judah arrived at Nehemiah's place: One hundred and fifty years after Babylon attacked Jerusalem, its walls were still broken and its gates burned. With the city in disrepair, Jews returning there from captivity were vulnerable to attack. They were in trouble. So was God's reputation. How could pagan nations respect him if he dwelt in a rubble heap?

The news grieved Nehemiah, and he immediately turned to God in prayer. This was no god created by man's imagination and molded by his hands. This was the God of heaven, the one whose hands created man. He spoke the universe into being with his words. He hung the stars in place and named them. In wisdom, he positioned the sun, moon, and earth and made four seasons to support life.

This was the God to whom Nehemiah prayed, and he did so with confidence. Jerusalem's repair was a God-sized task, so he called on the God of heaven—the one with unlimited wisdom, power, and resources—to make possible the impossible.

Ponder

What's the God-sized task or need facing you?

Pray

God, display your mighty wisdom and power. Draw from your unlimited resources to do the impossible.

"Through God's grace, he gives us a wealth of resources to bear any burden he allows. Therefore, if God doesn't empty our cup of suffering or take it from us, he will give ample grace (favor, kindness, ability) to bear it."

JENNIFER ROTHSCHILD,
God Is Just Not Fair: Finding Hope When Life Doesn't Make Sense

Humility

*The people you rescued by your great power
and strong hand are your servants. O Lord,
please hear my prayer! Listen to the prayers of
those of us who delight in honoring you.*

NEHEMIAH 1:10–11 NLT

$\mathcal{P}$*ause*

Nehemiah recognized that rebuilding Jerusalem required far more resources than he possessed or could muster. He prayed to God for help, but he didn't approach him with a "you allowed this mess to happen, so you owe me this" attitude. Instead, he approached God in humility.

Nehemiah acknowledged who God was, confessed the people's sins against him, and respectfully reminded him of his promises to restore his people (Nehemiah 1:5–10). Before he asked anything from God, he demonstrated a surrendered heart. He and the Jews were God's servants, and their role was to honor him.

We, too, need a humble heart when we come to the God of heaven for help. This means admitting our dependence on him because we don't have the resources to overcome the challenges we face. We're willing to trust his ways over our strategies. This is humility, and this is the quality God desires in all who ask him for aid. "God opposes the proud but gives grace to the humble" (1 Peter 5:5 NLT).

Ponder

What's your attitude and approach when you seek God's help?

Pray

God, I confess: you are God and I am not.

"A humble person is not one who thinks little of himself, hangs his head and says, 'I'm nothing.' Rather, he is one who depends wholly on the Lord for everything, in every circumstance."

DAVID WILKERSON,
"The Witness of the Spirit," *World Challenge*

Elijah Moments

The God of all grace, who called you to his eternal
glory in Christ, after you have suffered a little while,
will himself restore you and make you strong,
firm and steadfast.

1 PETER 5:10

Pause

The prophet Elijah teetered on the brink of burnout.
Exhausted after fleeing from Queen Jezebel, he collapsed
under a solitary tree and expressed a death wish.

At that moment, God could have rebuked him for allowing
fear to overrule faith. God could have told him to pull
his act together and return to business, but he did not.
Instead, God sent an angel with a jar of water and a
loaf of warm, homemade bread to feed and restore him
(1 Kings 19:5–7).

At some time or other, we might face an Elijah moment.
Hard times hit us and knock us flat. We're too weak to
stand up and stand firm, so we crawl into a ball and hide.
Our human nature tells us we're done.

But God is a gentle shepherd who cares tenderly for his weary lambs. He comes alongside to strengthen and restore us when we feel broken and battered. We might think we're done, but his purposes for us are not finished yet.

Ponder

How has God offered restoration for you in an Elijah moment?

Pray

God, thank you for sending Jesus—the bread of life and the living water—to restore and strengthen me.

"God does not say, '*If* you go through the fire' and flood and dark valleys but *when* you go. The promise is not that he will remove us from the experience of suffering. No, the promise is that God will be with us, walking beside us in it."

TIMOTHY KELLER,
Walking with God through Pain and Suffering

Hope in Heaven

Think about the things of heaven,
not the things of earth.

COLOSSIANS 3:2 NLT

Pause

Sailor-Man held the position of program director at a year-round Christian camp for a decade. When terminal cancer struck the executive director, Sailor-Man filled in the gap. He later applied for that position, and most everyone assumed he would get it. That's not what happened. The board hired a younger coworker instead.

Sailor-Man struggled with disappointment and a tinge of humiliation, but he responded with integrity and assisted the new director in his role for more than a year. They enjoyed friendship because Sailor-Man had long ago placed his hopes and dreams on things far more significant than a job position. He'd fixed his hopes on heaven, believing that the best is yet to come.

Earthly dreams we hold dear lose their luster in the light of heaven. So long as we're warm and breathing, we will face disappointments here. But not there. Heaven promises to heal hearts, satisfy souls, and surpass the wildest dreams our imagination can muster. When we feel discouraged and perhaps cast aside, let's keep our eyes on the prize. The best is yet to come.

Ponder

Where have you placed your hopes and dreams—on earth or in heaven?

Pray

God, you are my heart's desire. No earthly dream compares with knowing you.

"Perhaps disappointed dreams are our best opportunities to transfer hope to its rightful place. Heaven is where our biggest dreams belong. Realizing that can help us make it through the here and now without placing a burden on the present that it was never meant to bear."

PAULA RINEHART,
The Cleavers Don't Live Here Anymore: Making the Transition from Sixties Idealism to Nineties Realism

Choosin' Joy

Weeping may last through the night,
but joy comes with the morning.

PSALM 30:5 NLT

Pause

An online dictionary defines *perfect storm* as "a particularly bad or critical state of affairs, arising from a number of negative and unpredictable factors." This describes what happened to my friend Pam and her family.

First, a health issue forced her husband to resign from his long-time role as lead pastor. Then their youngest son was hospitalized for eight days with a serious football injury. Within days of his release, Pam's other two sons suffered athletic injuries and her younger brother was hospitalized with a heart attack. And so it continued.

Pam's perfect storm continued for three years. When people asked her how she was coping, she didn't know how to answer. One day she read Psalm 30:5 and the word *joy* caught her attention. She hunted for the word in Scripture, studied and printed the relevant verses, and hung them around her house. When others asked how she was doing, she began responding with, "Choosin' joy!"

What's your response when others ask how you're coping? I suspect that Pam—and the Lord—would be thrilled if you adopted "Choosin' joy!" as your answer.

Ponder

What word or phrase describes how you're doing today?

Pray

God, please empower me to choose joy, even when I don't feel joyful.

"Joy is the God-breathed wind in your sail
that navigates your life through
the storm to safe harbor."

PAM FARREL

Rock Climbing

With your help I can advance against a troop;
with my God I can scale a wall.

PSALM 18:29

Pause

My youngest daughter and her husband enjoy rock climbing. Listening to them talk about their favorite sport has taught me a new language. For instance, a belayer controls the rope attached to the climber and ensures protection should the climber fall. An anchor made of bolts, chains, slings, or ropes secures the belayer, thus adding another level of safety for the climber. An unquestionably safe anchor is called "bomb-proof."

Understanding these terms gives me a new appreciation for Psalm 18:29. A wall represents any challenge or obstacle we face. We needn't attempt to scale it single-handed, because God is with us and fulfills the belayer role. He knows everything about the wall we face and how best to climb it, and he uses his knowledge and skills to ensure victory.

The wall we face might be rugged and steep, but God holds us in his grip. We can trust him implicitly, just as my daughter and her husband trust each other on a climb. We need not fear, because his plan for helping us scale this obstacle is bomb-proof.

Ponder

How does envisioning God as your belayer bring confidence that you'll scale this wall successfully?

Pray

God, I choose to trust you with my life.

"If you are seeking to obey the Lord, expect opposition. Expect obstacles. Expect difficulties. But also expect God to see you through."

GREG LAURIE,
Beyond: A Devotional

Change Is Possible

For nothing will be impossible with God.

LUKE 1:37 ESV

Pause

I've prayed a specific request on a friend's behalf for more than three decades. My patience has worn a little thin at times, and I've wondered why God doesn't answer. *Am I asking amiss? Is my faith too small?* For a short stretch, I began losing hope, because I slipped into believing that change was impossible.

"Change is impossible" is a lie. Scripture teems with examples that prove the opposite is true, especially when God is involved. He changed chaos to order and darkness to light (Genesis 1:1–5). He changed fishermen's empty nets to bulging full of fish (John 21: 2–6). He changed blindness to 20/20 vision, and leprous sores to flawless skin (Mark 8:22–25; Matthew 8:2–3). Story after story assures us that anything is possible for the Lord.

God has proven his ability to change the impossible, but Satan will try to make us think otherwise. Believing his lie leads to lost hope. We'll eventually stop praying because, after all, there's no point.

My friend, do not give up. We don't know what God is doing or why our prayers seem to go unanswered, but we do know that the impossible is possible for him.

Ponder

What change do you desire most?

Pray

God, fill me with faith to believe change is possible.

"Nothing paralyzes our lives like the attitude that things can never change. We need to remind ourselves that God can change things!... Outlook determines outcome. If we see only the problems, we will be defeated; but if we see the possibilities in the problems, we can have victory."

WARREN W. WIERSBE,
The Bumps Are What You Climb On:
Encouragement for Difficult Days

Summon Courage

In the seventh year of Athaliah's reign, Jehoiada the priest decided to act. He summoned his courage and made a pact with five army commanders.

2 CHRONICLES 23:1 NLT

Pause

Jehoiada and his wife rescued Joash, their infant nephew, from death at the hands of his despot grandmother. Seven years later, God compelled Jehoiada to overthrow the evil matriarch and appoint Joash as the throne's rightful heir. Taking action meant mustering his courage to face the unknowns head-on.

Our battles—both relational and situational ones—intimidate us, and fear says each battle is too big. Retreat beckons, but we needn't bow to its bidding, because God has given us everything we need to do battle and overcome our enemy. We begin by summoning our courage. How? By living from the truth: "for God did not give us a spirit of timidity or cowardice or fear, but [He has given us a spirit] of power and of love and of sound judgment and personal discipline [abilities that result in a calm, well-balanced mind and self-control] (2 Timothy 1:7 AMP).

Summon your courage, my friend. God is on your side. He will guide you and strengthen you. He has made you a warrior equipped for battle.

Ponder

For what do you need to summon courage?

Pray

God, fill me with courage and lead me as I confront this battle.

"When you accept the fact that your true identity includes being an overcomer, you will never settle for less than a miracle."

CRAIG GROESCHEL,
Altar Ego: Becoming Who God Says You Are

Thankful in the Storm

*After [Paul] said this, he took some bread
and gave thanks to God in front of them all.
Then he broke it and began to eat.*

ACTS 27:35

Pause

Today's verse sounds so uneventful, but don't let it fool you. We find it sandwiched between Paul's two-week voyage through a hurricane-like storm and his being shipwrecked on an island.

It's easy to give thanks to God when the winds calm and the waves settle. Anyone can sigh words of gratitude when dawn replaces darkness. But it takes a special sort to thank God when knowingly facing a shipwreck. First Peter 4:13 (NLT) explains why we ought to strive to belong in that special category: "Instead, be very glad—for these trials make you partners with Christ in his suffering, so that you will have the wonderful joy of seeing his glory when it is revealed to all the world."

We give thanks, not for the suffering that lies ahead, but because we're promised wonderful joy in it and afterwards. Someday we'll see Christ's glory, and then our pain will have been all worthwhile. For that we give thanks, and we choose to persevere.

Ponder

For what can you give thanks today?

Pray

God, make me thankful for suffering as the portal through which I will glimpse your glory.

> "I have learned that in every circumstance that comes my way, I can choose to respond in one of two ways: I can *whine* or I can *worship!* And I can't worship without giving thanks. It just isn't possible. When we choose the pathway of worship and giving thanks, especially in the midst of difficult circumstances, there is a fragrance, a radiance, that issues forth out of our lives to bless the Lord and others."
>
> NANCY DEMOSS WOLGEMUTH, WITH LAWRENCE KIMBROUGH, *Choosing Gratitude: Your Journey to Joy*

God Speaks

My sheep listen to my voice;
I know them, and they follow me.

JOHN 10:27

Pause

"This is the day, this is the day that the Lord has made."
These lyrics from Matt Johnson's song assumed new
meaning for me under unusual circumstances. It
happened one afternoon when Sailor-Man mowed the
lawn on a piece of property we owned. He'd taken our
two preschoolers with him, and I planned to join them after
our sleeping infant woke from her nap.

Unfortunately, Sailor-Man's sneakered left foot slipped
under the lawnmower. Minus three toes, he managed to
lie down and yell to the closest neighbor for help. As he
waited for assistance, our four-year-old son planted himself
by his daddy's head and began to sing in his best voice:
"This is the day, this is the day that the Lord has made." The
lyrics encouraged all within earshot to rejoice and be glad.

Personally, I wanted to wish that day away, but God spoke to my heart through my child's singing. God reminded me that he reigns over every day. Nothing happens that takes him by surprise or leaves him panicked. He conveyed his message loud and clear. Three decades later, I still hear those lyrics reminding me of that truth, especially on difficult days.

Ponder

What truth has a child's innocent remark taught you?

Pray

God, speak to me using any method you want, and I will listen.

> "God can use the words of a teenager,
> the prayer of a senior citizen, or the candid
> remark of a child to convict you of the need
> to make changes in your life."
>
> HENRY BLACKABY AND RICHARD BLACKABY,
> *Hearing God's Voice*

Soul Care

The elders of his household stood beside him to get
him up from the ground, but he refused, and he
would not eat any food with them.

2 SAMUEL 12:17

Pause

Two days after my mother's passing, my brother and his wife invited me and Sailor-Man to attend a Sunday morning church service with them. Sailor-Man said yes; I said, "No, thanks." This was the church Mom had attended. It was also my church for the first eighteen years of my life. One might have thought I'd welcome familiar faces in my time of loss, but the opposite was true. More than sympathy, my soul needed alone time with God, my Bible, my journal, and a good cup of coffee.

King David knew his soul's deepest need as his infant son lay dying. More than food and fellowship, David craved intimacy with God. When his well-meaning friends urged him to eat with them, he said no.

People who genuinely care will offer advice when they see us hurt. In some cases, their advice is warranted because they see something to which we're blind. In other cases, it's okay to say "No, thanks" and do what you know is best for your soul in that moment.

Ponder

What does your soul need right now?

Pray

God, help me discern what my soul needs to be healthy.

"Everyone wanted me to get help and rejoin life,
pick up the pieces and move on, and I tried to,
I wanted to, but I just had to lie in the mud with
my arms wrapped around myself, eyes closed,
grieving, until I didn't have to anymore.
And then over time I became more or less okay;
I did feel joy again, and I feel it now sometimes
bigger than I ever thought possible."

ANNE LAMOTT, *Operating Instructions:
A Journal of My Son's First Year*

Moving Forward

*Then David got up from the ground. After he had
washed, put on lotions and changed his clothes,
he went into the house of the LORD and worshiped.
Then he went to his own house, and at his request
they served him food, and he ate.*

2 SAMUEL 12:20

Pause

King David did not linger in his place of pain after his baby
died. He rose from the floor, cleaned himself, worshiped
the Lord, and then went home to eat. He understood that
he could neither change the outcome nor return to life as
it was. God had answered his prayer with a firm no, and
David surrendered to God's ways, not with an attitude of
doomed resignation, but with worship.

Sometimes we linger in our place of pain. We hang on,
hoping God will reverse our circumstances. We're unable
to let go and unwilling to accept change. We want what
was, and we're afraid of what might be. We will languish
in that place unless we move forward.

God is God and we are not. Surrendering to his ways gives us the strength to get up. Worship enables us to take the necessary steps to move forward. He holds our hand all the way.

Ponder

I worship God today because he is _____.

Pray

God, I choose not to linger and languish. I get up because of who you are.

> "When we don't understand, like or agree with the way life has gone, we are to bow before God and once again confess that we can't understand His wisdom and knowledge. In faith, we are to accept His wisdom, His Word, and His workings, trusting in Him and obeying His commands ... even in the dark."
>
> ELIZABETH GEORGE,
> *Loving God with All Your Mind*

How Will the Story End?

When Joseph's brothers saw that their father
was dead, they said, "What if Joseph holds
a grudge against us and pays us back
for all the wrongs we did to him?"

GENESIS 50:15

Pause

As readers today, we hold a distinct advantage over Joseph and his brothers. We can open our Bibles and read a play-by-play, knowing their story concludes with a happy ending—forgiveness reigns and their family reconciles—but they weren't privy to that information as their lives unfolded.

Joseph may have faced more than a few uncertain moments as he sat fettered in prison. Would he live or die? His brothers may have wondered the same thing about their future as they considered the possibility of Joseph seeking revenge after their father's death.

We don't know how our story will play out because God doesn't reveal tomorrow's events today or give us a sneak peek. But here's something we do know for sure: God authors every chapter of our life. He pens the plots that twist and turn, and he leads them to a conclusion that's best in his eyes and written with competency. It might not read as we wish, but it will always be better than what we might have imagined.

Ponder

If you could write the conclusion for your current life chapter, what would it look like?

Pray

God, I trust you as the author of my story.

"You do not need to know precisely what is happening, or exactly where it is all going. What you need is to recognize the possibilities and challenges offered by the present moment, and to embrace them with courage, faith, and hope."

THOMAS MERTON,
Conjectures of a Guilty Bystander

Holy Spirit Helper

*The Advocate, the Holy Spirit, whom the Father will
send in my name, will teach you all things and will
remind you of everything I have said to you.*

JOHN 14:26

Pause

Knowing that his crucifixion was imminent, Jesus poured instruction and encouragement into his disciples. He knew about the hardships they would face after his departure, and he wanted to ensure they were equipped for what was to come. He went above and beyond in this endeavor.

Jesus provided his followers with an advocate—someone to support them and come alongside as a helper. He said that, among other tasks, the Holy Spirit would remind them of his words and teach them all things.

The Spirit did exactly what Jesus promised. He empowered a dozen ordinary men to change the world with the gospel as they listened to his voice and followed his lead.

The Holy Spirit is our advocate, too, but sometimes we forget about him. We try to handle our hardships on our own, but that rarely works well. Remembering his presence in us makes all the difference. He'll empower us as we listen to him and follow his lead.

Ponder

With what would you like the Holy Spirit to help you?

Pray

God, make me mindful of the Holy Spirit's presence and power in me.

> "The Holy Spirit is interceding for us with groans
> that cannot be uttered. Long before we woke up
> this morning and long after we go to sleep tonight,
> the Holy Spirit was and is circling us in prayer.
> And if that doesn't infuse us with holy confidence,
> I don't know what will."
>
> MARK BATTERSON,
> *Draw the Circle: The 40 Day Prayer Challenge*

Outweighed

*For our present troubles are small and won't last
very long. Yet they produce for us a glory that vastly
outweighs them and will last forever!*

2 CORINTHIANS 4:17 NLT

Pause

While in Egypt, Sailor-Man and I bought bananas from
a street vendor. The man used an old balance scale
to determine the fruit's weight, so he could charge me
accordingly. He set the fruit on one side of the instrument
and then placed small lead weights on the opposite side
until the scale balanced. He completed his calculations
in a matter of seconds.

That fellow's job was an easy one compared to a
measurement mentioned in God's Word. Imagine placing
our present troubles on one side of a balance scale. The
weight instantly drops the plate to the surface below. On
the opposite side of the balance, let's place the eternal
glory that we will experience as a result of the troubles
God allows in our lives. What happens? The glory's weight
proves greater.

Our troubles weigh heavy, but eternal glory weighs more. This is the truth about the difficulties we face, no matter what they look like. God said it is so, and it *is* so.

Ponder

What's one spiritual truth you're learning through your present situation?

Pray

God, help me remember that eternal glory always outweighs my troubles.

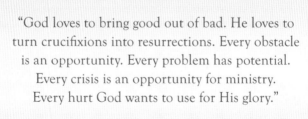

"God loves to bring good out of bad. He loves to turn crucifixions into resurrections. Every obstacle is an opportunity. Every problem has potential. Every crisis is an opportunity for ministry. Every hurt God wants to use for His glory."

RICK WARREN

Meet Grace

Grace is a devotional blogger, member of the First 5 writing team (Proverbs 31 Ministries), and popular speaker at women's retreats and conferences internationally.

Her passion is to connect the dots between faith and real life by helping her audiences learn to love, understand, and apply God's Word for life transformation. Besides writing and speaking, she's a career global worker and enjoys training others for short-term and career missions. She and her husband live on a sailboat near Vancouver, British Columbia.

Be sure to read the first devotional in this series: *Finding Hope in Crisis: Devotions for Calm in Chaos.*

www.gracefox.com
grace@gracefox.com
www.fb.com/gracefox.author